ISBN 978-1-333-18513-8
PIBN 10660119

1 MONTH OF
FREE
READING

at

www.ForgottenBooks.com

By purchasing this book you are eligible for one month membership to ForgottenBooks.com, giving you unlimited access to our entire collection of over 1,000,000 titles via our web site and mobile apps.

To claim your free month visit:

www.forgottenbooks.com/free660119

ANTHROPOLOGICAL REPORT

ON THE

EDO-SPEAKING PEOPLES OF NIGERIA.

PART I: LAW AND CUSTOM.

BY

NORTHCOTE W. THOMAS, M.A., F.R.A.I., ETC.

GOVERNMENT ANTHROPOLOGIST.

———

LONDON:

HARRISON AND SONS.

——

1910.

CONTENTS.

		PAGE.
SECTION I.—LANGUAGE AND PEOPLE		5
,, II.—RELIGION AND MAGIC		24
,, III.—MARRIAGE AND BIRTH		47
,, IV.—INHERITANCE, ADOPTION AND PROPERTY		64
,, V.—LAW		103
,, VI.—KINSHIP		112

APPENDICES :—

(A) LINGUISTICS		123
(B) GENEALOGIES AND KINSHIP		138
(C) PHOTOGRAPHIC AND PHONOGRAPHIC RECORDS		153
INDEX		161

A map showing the distribution of Edo-speaking peoples and neighbouring regions. Labelled areas and places include:

AKOKO — Kabb, Okpe, Aroko, Egpese, Otua

IGBIRA — Sosa, Usua, Ibilo, Gan, Semolika, Lokoj

UPILA — Kofunno, Okpe

IBIE — Opepe, Yayg, Ikbe, Ugaibui, Fuga, Auci, Isoka, Isebe, Woriki

KUKURUKU — Ejeba, Afuji, Sabon gida, Ororo, Idua, Jegbe, Edo, Agbede, Uzia, Idegun, Ewu, Ama, Ewori

ORA — IFON, Igiawe

RIVER NIGER — Yonipadi, Egor, Agenibodi

IGARA — IDA, Boundary of Edo speaking peoples

ISHAN — Edela, Irua, Ako, Uromi, Idumibo, Jeduma, Ubiaja, Jigola, Agbor

IBO — Asc, Onitsha

IKA — Agbor

EDO — Ojogbo, Iguchimi, Iyowa, Utekon, Idumowina, Eviekoi, Ugo, EDO (City of Benin), Gwaton, Usen, Okolo

YORUBA — Sapele, Amukpe

Inset map of NIGERIA showing NORTHERN, WESTERN, and SOUTHERN PROVINCE regions, with BENIN, CENTRAL PROVINCE, EASTERN PROVINCE, CALABAR, and CADUCAR.

SECTION I.

Language and People.

Area.—The group of peoples with which the present report is concerned occupies the centre and north-east of the central province of Southern Nigeria, and a portion of the southern part of the Kabba province. The area is roughly oval in shape, with its long axis north and south and of a maximum length of some hundred and fifty miles, and a short axis of sixty miles or less. The most southerly point appears to be south-east of Warri, and the most northerly point a few miles north of a line running from Isua to Ibilo.

In this area is one large tribe, the Edo or Bini, of which Edo, as they themselves term it, or Benin City, is the capital; north-east of them lie the Esa or Ishans round Ubiaja; south of them lie the Sobo, with three or more dialects; and the remainder of the area is taken up with a mass of tribes, some of them limited to a single village, which are sometimes collectively known as Kukuruku. In the south-west of the Kukuruku country we have the Ora country, and further to the east, north of the Esa, are the districts of Uzaitui, Fuga, and Agenigbodi. Over the border, in Northern Nigeria, are the Ibie and Upila districts; in each of these districts the language appears to be fairly homogeneous; outside them the linguistic groups are often exceedingly small; in the north-east angle of the Ifon District, for example, we find Iki, Aroko, Otua, and Okpe, the languages of which are said to be mutually unintelligible, though they are not more than two hours distant from each other.

PHYSICAL TYPE.—There is little uniformity of physical type among the Edo-speaking peoples, though it is not difficult to recognise a Sobo or an Edo. The average stature of the men appears to be about five feet five inches. As regards physical strength there is also much variation, if the performances of carriers can be taken as a criterion; though it must be remembered that a carrier living on strange food and traversing unusual ground cannot approach his normal performances. Generally speaking the hill people are superior in physique to the people of the plains, and will carry equal loads in spite of the difference of ground. Although the negro is able to carry loads for long distances, he must go at his own pace; even without a load his endurance is small when he is called upon to move faster than usual.

As a rule, malnutrition is rare; but occasionally, as in the Ora country, there is a lack of food owing to sheer laziness.

Tribal marks and fashions in hairdressing are now losing their significance, but the raised scar on the forehead of the Sobo, the crow's foot at the outer angle of the eye in the Ishan, and a few more are yet kept up.

Physical deformities are rarely seen, the main one to catch the eye being umbilical hernia, due to wrong methods at birth; it is very local in its distribution.

Lunacy is rare; deaf and dumb people are occasionally met with. Among abnormalities may be mentioned albinism (common in places), red hair (rare), and supernumerary fingers.

LANGUAGE.—The family of languages whose distribution is here described appears to be distinct from those of the surrounding peoples, which are, on the south the Ijọ; on the west the Yoruba, on the north-west and north tribes of the Yoruba stock, on the north-east the Igbira; on the east, but on the other bank of the Niger, are the Igara at Ida; then come, on the west bank of the Niger, various branches of the Ibo, who extend down into the Ijọ territory.

Certain words appear to be common to the Edo and other

families of languages, but in some cases their prevalence in both families can be readily explained; and in any case their number is far too few to afford the presumption of any relation between the languages, whose syntax appears to be entirely different. If there is any resemblance between the Edo family and other West African languages, it is probably to be found with the Ewe tribes of Togoland and the Gold Coast, with the verbal forms of which there are certain obvious resemblances.

Among the words common to Edo and Yoruba are such terms as oke (hill), okuta (stone), and the like, and the reason for their appearance in both families of languages is firstly, that the line of kings which formerly ruled the Edo came from the Ife country; and that, secondly, hills and stones being virtually unknown in the Edo country, terms for them would naturally be adopted from the language of the immigrants.

There are certain resemblances between the Edo and Ibo languages which are more difficult to explain. Parts of the body for example, like the mouth (unu), are known by identical names, and here it is difficult to suggest an explanation. Finally, there are a certain number of words, like ekuiye (spoon), which are obviously adopted from a romance language of Europe, and we need have no difficulty on deciding on Portuguese as their source, for it is well known that the Portuguese were in Edo at the beginning of the sixteenth century.

The languages are, as a rule, difficult to learn or understand, and the difficulties arise from two sources. In the first place, a sentence or phrase coalesces into a single word with the vowels elided or euphonic letters inserted. It is often difficult to discover from an interpreter what are the words which are the component parts of such a phrase.

In the second place, the Edo languages are, like Yoruba, and certain other West African languages, toned, that is to say, the meaning of monosyllables, dissyllables, and sometimes of even longer words, is changed by altering the intonation with which they are spoken. To take a simple example, ehá means three, while ĕha means six; in this case stress and accent coincide. To take a more complicated example, Idĕ means "I come," while Îde means "I am not coming." Idè means "I buy," Idé means "I fall," and Ide, "I tie." When toned words are included in the body of an agglutinative word, the difficulty of recognition, which is sometimes considerable in any case, is greatly increased.

In Edo proper there is, as a rule, no plural, but a certain number of words change an initial o into i to form the plural, thus:—oxwo, ixwo, woman; odiǫñ, elder; idiǫñ, elder. The pronoun commonly used for the third person, namely, ǫna, or ǫ, is inflected in the same way, and has plural ina, or a. Many nouns are in reality the third person singular of a verb, as, for example, ǫmaxe (he makes pots), potter; plural, imaxe. But it would be erroneous to suppose that the plural of non-verbal nouns has been formed by analogy from that of verbal nouns; for, in a few cases in Edo, we find plural in e, for example, ǫbo, doctor; ǫbo, doctors; in the second place, in some of the Kukuruku languages, other vowels undergo a change. The vowel in the plural is sometimes a: for example, obǫ, hand; abǫ, hands, in Ishan.

The personal pronouns are in Edo i, ti, me, or memo for the first person, we for the second person, sometimes found in the form u before gb, w, etc.; for the third person, ǫna, ǫ, oi, le, e, etc. In the plural, ma, wa, and ina. Personal pronouns are prefixed to the verb, which is uninflected for a person or tense. The objective pronoun usually follows the verb, but is occasionally inserted in the body of the word. An example of the former is inele from ine, I know, le, it; an example of the latter, inome, I do not marry; inelomi, I do not marry him.

In connection with this latter example, attention may be called to a peculiarity of some of these languages. There is no negative in inome, but a particle must be inserted to change the verb from negative to positive. Thus: iganome means "I am going to marry."

A particle ga inserted after the personal pronoun, is the normal method of forming the future, for the perfect ne may be affixed to the stem of the verb, or fo (*i.e.*, finished) may be used in the same way. Thus: iluc, I do it; igalue, I shall do it; iluene or iluefo, I have done it.

The negative may be indicated in various ways. The accent may be thrown back as in idé, I come; íde, I am not coming, or ma may be inserted in the stem of the verb; for example, imadẹ̀, I do not buy. For the negative imperative ge is used—for example, gemudia, do not stop. The subject pronoun precedes the verb in the interrogative sense, and the question is shown by a particle, by dynamic stress, or by musical intonation. Thus ugbẽ means you killed him; ŭgbe, did you (not) kill him?

Subórdinate sentences are comparatively rare. The relative pronoun is ne, and relative sentences are frequent. Subordinate sentences of time are also found, but the ordinary method of expressing a hypothetical clause is to make it co-ordinate with the main sentence. Thus, to express in Edo " If you stay I will stay," one says, wamudia (you stay) idiake (I stay with you).

In connection with the verb mention must be made of the importance of separable verbs, thus: mure, bring, mọrukpare, bring the lamp; another feature is the piling up of verbs to express what is to us a simple idea. Thus: irhiegade, I bring, is compounded from irie, I take; ga, go; de, come.

A certain number of impersonal verbs are found, usually of sensations or emotions, thus: ohamegbime, I am thirsty.

The adjective is uninflected, except for comparison, of which there is only one degree, formed by adding se, past, thus: ọkpalo, big; ọkpalọse, bigger.

There are distinct words in all the Edo languages for numbers from one to ten, twenty, sometimes thirty, and two hundred. The numbers from eleven to twenty are compounded in two ways: from twenty upwards they are vicesimal with the exception of thirty, the term for which is sometimes borrowed from the Yoruba.

	Edo.	Aroko.	Otua.	Sobo of Iyede.	Kukuruku of Uzairui.	Ishan.
1.	Ǫkpa, owo	ǫkpa	ǫkpa	ǫvo…	ǫkpa	Ǫkpa.
2.	eva	era	eva…	ive …	eva	era.
3.	ehã	eha	esa …	ǫrha, esa	ea	ea.
4.	ine	ene	ene …	ene …	edi	ine.
5.	ise	ihi	ize …	inyoli	ise	iseñi.
6.	ẍha	isesa	izeza	esã …	esa	eta.
7.	ihino	ihinia	izinia	iwule	iselua	ilhino.
8.	elele	iniene	enie	ẽlele	ele	ilǫlǫ.
9.	ihini	isini	isi …	izili…	iči	isini.
10.	igbe	igbe	igbe	ikwe	igbe	igbe.
11.	ǫwǫrǫ	igbokpa	igbokpa	iwǫvo	igbeloa	igbǫloa.
12.	iweva[1]	igbeva	igbeva	iwive	igbeva	igbeva.
13.	iwera	igbeva	igbesa	iwera	igbelea	igbeá.
14.	iwene	igbene	igbene	iwene	igbedi	igbene.
15.	ikesugie	igbilhi	igbize	ixwioli	igbese	igbehǫle.
16.	enelawugie	ikainerasue	azenezowige	ixwesa, ixwioligbǫvo	igbelesa	okpai igbehǫle.
17.	ehalawugie	ikaiairasue	azesazowige	ixwioligbive	igbeselua	eva igbehǫle.
18.	evarawugie	ikevaresue	azevasowige	ixwiolerha…	igbele	era igbehǫle.
19.	ǫkpadewugie	ikǫkparesue	azǫkpasowige	ixwiolene	igbeči	ine igbehǫle.
20.	ugie	uwe	owige	uže…	uwe	ue.

[1] From a form iwo ; cf. Ewe ęwo.

VILLAGE.—Villages vary in size from the hamlet of three or four houses, and twenty or thirty inhabitants, to places with a thousand or more inhabitants, which are themselves only quarters of a larger town. Especially in the hill country, we find large populations, perhaps as many as ten thousand in some places, in a small area, recognising the authority of one head chief.

SOCIAL ORGANISATION.—The organisation of the village varies with the tribe; in the Edo country there is a tripartite division of the males—senior grade is known as Idiǫñ, or elders, next to them comes Igele, and the junior grade is known as the Ologai.

The Idiǫñ are virtually the council of the village, and in pre-European times they dealt with minor law cases, the more important ones being sent to Edo for the judgment of the king.

The Igele, assisted as a rule by some of the junior Idiǫñ, have to undertake such work as roofing houses, and it is from this rank that carriers are usually drawn.

The Ologai carry wood and water, and do some of the work of cleaning the roads. A boy joins this rank as soon as he is strong enough. The promotion from the Igele to the Idiǫñ is obtained by means of payment.

It is difficult to say what the average proportions of the various grades are, but in a total population of about one thousand I obtained the following figures: Idiǫñ, one hundred and eighty-one; Igele, fifty-eight; Ologai, seventy-five.

The villages of the Edo country were grouped, before the European occupation, some under princes who were known as Ogie (plural Igie), others under chiefs, stewards, or other heads. The Igie were descendants of former kings, whom custom compelled to live away from the capital. Each village, whether presided over by an Ogie or not, was represented in Edo by a chief or king's steward, and communications to the king were normally made through this representative. Tribute in kind was paid to the king, a proportion of which was retained by the representative.

In the Ora country, and the greater portion of the Kukuruku country, the adult males of the village who have not attained to chieftainship, are organised in companies (Otu) formed of men of about the same age. An Otu is inaugurated, as a rule, once in three years, and, as a rule the junior Otu has to undertake the cleaning of the roads. Where there is no lack of labour, the senior Otu are dispensed from labour, and the four junior Otu do the work, with one Otu to supervise them. The commencement of a new Otu is celebrated with more or less festivity, and in some places they wear ceremonial dresses and dance round the town in the same way as Secret Societies.

The various Otu are known by names, by collecting which on a large scale it is possible to arrive at some idea of the average age of the oldest men of a village.

As a rule, the oldest Otu in a place of any size appears to be about forty years older than the junior Otu. If they come in once in three years, the oldest men who have not yet become chiefs must be about sixty-five years of age.

In the Ishan country, the organisation comes nearer the Edo tribe. In Irua, they have two Otu, of which the senior is liable for work only when there is much to be done. Above the Otu come the Igele and the Idiọñ.

Elsewhere in the Ishan country only Idiọñ and Igele are found.

In the Sobo country the social organisation is more rudimentary, but there is a division into old men, adults, and small boys. The adult men are often spoken of as a " Club," over which there is a headman.

In the kingdom of Edo there were in pre-European times two kinds of chiefs, a small number of the more important were succeeded by their sons, but, as a rule, a position was sold by the king for the highest figure. A son of the late chief was not necessarily excluded, but he had no special claim to his father's position.

In the Kukuruku country at the present day the position of chief is purchased, and the payment goes to the existing body of chiefs; in the Ora country the cost appears to be comparatively small; and in the kingdom of Agbede, where there is a king, chieftainship appears to be a comparatively minor matter. In Ida, however, and probably in the adjacent parts of Northern Nigeria, the cost of becoming a chief is heavy (about £30), and the system gives rise to grave abuses.

Originally there was considerable advantage attaching to the position of chief, for he could neither be arrested nor attacked in war. At the present day, the only advantage of becoming a chief, if we except a certain amount of prestige attaching to the position, appears to be the share in the fees of the new chiefs, which is squandered in riotous living. So far as I could discover, practically the whole of the fees are paid in kind, and the payments are spread over a period of years. Each payment appears to be an excuse for a feast on the part of the recipients, and the only result of the present system is to impoverish the community.

By limiting the number of chiefs a check would be put upon this waste, greatly to the advantage of the people at large; or, alternatively, it might be possible to enact that a proportion of the fees payable by the new chiefs should be handed over to the Government for the benefit of the community.

In the Sobo country women chiefs are found, and the system by which chiefs are chosen appears to vary considerably. In some cases chieftainship is hereditary, in others it depends upon age, and in others upon wealth.

DEMOGRAPHY.—It is commonly assumed that in Africa generally women far outnumber the men. I collected statistics from four contiguous villages in the neighbourhood of Edo by the genealogical method. In the nature of things, no exact statistics as to age are available, but, assuming that all the youths above the Ologai are adults, and that all women of the same age or older are married, the proportions of the sexes are almost precisely equal. In point of fact, a certain number of Ologai are married, and it appears there-lore that the males above the age of puberty are more numerous than the females, for there are a certain number of unmarried males, whereas only such females as are widows or too old to marry again, remain unmarried above the age of puberty.

In addition to enumerating the adults, I also recorded the names of all the children. It is necessary to make special enquiry as to the number of children who are dead. The infant mortality appears to be enormous, and children who die soon after birth are so often omitted in the genealogies that the statistics are quite misleading. It may be added that it is also necessary to make special enquiries about deceased wives; it frequently happens that their names are omitted, and their children may be passed over.

In the villages in question, taking children of all ages, or rather all the descendants of those now living in the villages, I found two hundred and twenty-eight males to one hundred and eighty-three females.

In order to discover the exact meaning of these figures, it is necessary to discover how many of them are of the age of two years or less. At the time of recording genealogies, when my figures were not yet tabulated, I did not realise the necessity for this. Accordingly, it is impossible to say whether a surplus of males runs right through the population up to the age of puberty, or whether more males are born than females, and the male mortality is greater than the female. The question is further complicated by the fact that many of the younger males leave the village to work on concessions. If their names are omitted in the enumeration, the apparent equality between the sexes in adult life, which is inexplicable, if the statistics from descendants are accurate, is readily explained. It must, however, be admitted that the numbers recorded in the genealogies are in any case too small to give a thoroughly reliable result.

In order to test the results thus obtained, I have tabulated the sexes of the descendants of the older generation, that is to say, of the brothers and sisters of the people now living in the village, who are not descendants of people still alive, and, where I could obtain the information, I have included the figures of their descendants. It must, however, be remembered (a) that there is a tendency to forget the names and sexes of children who die soon after birth, where the informant is not one of the parents ; and (b) that the numbers of the women in particular are apt to be too small, because, where the information is drawn from the youngest son of a family, the names of the elder sisters may be either unknown to him or forgotten. This was clearly shown by the statistics of the sex of the first-born child ; for, whereas in the present generation, the proportions were seventy-nine males to fifty-five females, including only those cases in which the children were still alive, the proportion in the earlier generation was forty-seven males to nineteen females. The total of the earlier generation was one hundred and three males and sixty females.

I obtained apparently reliable statistics as to the death rate for about one-half the total number of families. The total number of living descendants of people residing in Utekon was one hundred and ninety-six, and the total number of deaths of their descendants, almost all of them in infancy, was one hundred and twenty-nine, giving a death rate of about four hundred per thousand. As some of the living were infants, it may be assumed that not far off five hundred children out of a thousand die.

In the four villages enumerated the average number of living wives of a husband was 1·5, including deceased wives and those who had eloped it is 1·7. Of a grand total of two hundred and forty males, one hundred and fifty-five were married, and no information was obtainable as to ten. More than two-fifths of the married men had two wives, and one-fifth had three wives.

The average number of children per husband, including only those who remain alive, was 2·7 ; including all children alive and dead, the average number of children becomes 2·7 per wife, and 4·5 per husband.

I did not record genealogies on a sufficiently large scale elsewhere to give reliable results, but in one of the compounds of Fuga I found an excess of females over males, the exact figures being seventy-eight males and ninety-three females.

A fragment taken from another compound showed a small excess of males. I also recorded the number and sexes of the children in the older generation, as in the Edo country, and here, for some reason, the total numbers recorded were considerably greater. Among them, however, were included all the children of women of the present generation who had married out of the compound. The totals thus gained gave two hundred and three males to a hundred and sixty-five females. The proportions obtained by combining these numbers with those already given, suggests that in Fuga the sexes are about equal in number.

If the figures drawn from the Edo villages and from Fuga are even approximately correct they are somewhat difficult to explain. It is a well-established fact that privation and hardship tend to produce an excess of male births. But life in the old days was undoubtedly harder than it is at present, and there can be little doubt, that life in the Edo country is easier than life in the Kukuruku country. Statistics, however, on a much larger scale, are needed in order to give reliable results.

In the Sobo country genealogies were persistently falsified to make the number of children appear as small as possible. I obtained reliable statistics in one village only; and they showed 3·5 living children per marriage, which was usually monogamous.

Food.—In connection with the genealogies, I also made enquiries as to the amount of property possessed by each man. As might be expected, movable property, other than food products, was comparatively rare in the villages. The statistics of yam production showed that the output varied enormously, according to the industry or otherwise of the labourer. Yams are stacked in ropes (Uga) of twenty-two or twenty-three, ten ropes make an Ekbo, or stack. In some cases an adult man, unmarried, did not produce more than five Uga, while others, under no more favourable conditions, produced five Ekbo. On an average, each adult man appears to produce about two Ekbo, or four hundred and fifty yams. The total output for the three villages where the enquiry was made was about a hundred and seventy-nine Ekbo. The adult population was about one hundred and eighty, and there were the same number of children. It must, however, be remembered that in a certain number of cases men were sick and unable to work their farms. Had this not been the case about twenty more Ekbo would probably have been produced.

Yams are the staple food of the Edo proper, but, as these statistics show, they must be largely eked out by other products, such as corn, beans, and koko yams, which are not included in the figures given above.

In the hill country of Otua and Okpe far more corn appears to be produced, and it is common to find large corn-fields quite close to a quarter. I found it, however, impossible to obtain statistics as to the annual output.

The staple food of the Sobo country is cassava. Here again, though from a different reason, it was impossible to give accurate figures ; whereas yams are dug up and stacked as soon as they are ripe, cassava may be, and is, left in the ground for a considerable period. I measured some of the crops which were worked by individual families, from which it appeared that the area for adults was about two hundred square feet. The statistics were collected on a small scale, and it was impossible to say what the total output of cassava for this area would be.

As a rule, the yam stacks of a village in the Edo country are found on the farms themselves, elsewhere they are frequently in the bush, and only chance, or information from an inhabitant of the place, will disclose the locality. As a rule, yams are brought to the village each day in quantities sufficient for consumption.

Corn is stacked in conical piles with a pole in the centre. These stacks appear to be made, as a rule, on the farms.

In addition to yams, cassava, and corn, banana and plantain are found in most parts. Many different sorts of bean are grown, and in the Sobo and Kukuruku countries, and to a less extent in other parts, a considerable amount of dried fish appears to be eaten. Flesh appears to be but seldom consumed. Eggs and milk are unknown as articles of diet.

The only intoxicating liquor produced over a great part of this area is palm wine, made from the oil palm by (*a*) a cut below the crown, or (*b*) by felling the tree; another kind is produced from *raphia vinifera*. Where guinea corn is common *pito* is made from it.

CALENDAR.—Although an enquiry as to the age of a man in years, or the number of years since a given event, will meet with no answer or a random one, a calendar year is known to all the Edo-speaking people. In the kingdom of Edo, two kinds of years were known, male and female, one of which was probably about a month longer than the other.

The year was divided into months, or, as they are usually termed, moons. In most cases they have no name, in other cases, as in Edo itself, the only names which are known do not stand in any exact relation to the lunar months, but are taken from the ceremonies proper to certain periods of the year. Occasionally, months other than lunar months are known, and at one point in Northern Nigeria, a twenty-day month seems to be used, with two periods of nine months to our year.

The week is everywhere a recognised period of time, and is, properly speaking, four days long, this being the interval between the two markets at any given spot. Occasionally, as in the Ida district, eight-day markets are found, but the names applied to the intervening days clearly show that a four-day week was the primary one.

One of the four days is commonly known as the rest-day

and on this day men frequently stop at home, though farm work is not absolutely forbidden. Women, on the other hand, go to market as usual.

MARKET.—The hour for the market varies in different parts of the country, in the kingdom of Edo and in the Sobo country it begins in the forenoon, and is fullest about mid-day, and the same appears to be the case with the markets in the Kaba province. At Agbede, on the other hand, markets are held in the afternoon, and about three o'clock is the hour at which the market-place is full.

Hausa and Yoruba traders apart, market trading is entirely in the hands of women, and the products which are set out for sale in the market are, as usual in Africa, almost ex-clusively food-stuff.

In addition to the market, there is the so-called silent trade. Outside a village may often be seen by the wayside, plantains or other eatables with palm kernels lying near them. These are for sale, and the palm kernels indicate the price in cowries.

With the exception of the gates of Edo itself, there appear to have been no points at which tolls were collected. At the gates of Edo, in pre-European times, the gate-keepers are said to have collected five cowries from each person going to market, or, according to another account, five per cent. of the value of the load.

To the question whether a village with an established market had a right to object to the setting up of another market on the same day in the same neighbourhood I could never get a definite answer. The formalities which attend the setting up of a market are slight, and, on the whole, it appeared that a new market set up under such conditions would probably not attract a sufficient number of people, and that therefore the experiment would probably not be tried.

The market-place is sometimes wholly within the territory of the village, though it is not necessarily anywhere near an inhabited centre. In other places the market-place is neutral ground, standing midway between two villages, or upon the boundary of their territories. In former times, the seizing of pawns in the market-place or on the way to market was forbidden, and any place which declined to conform to this regulation was unable to carry on a market.

In the present day, holding of the market is largely dependent upon the supply of food-stuff, and, in the time of scarcity, before the new yams come in, it may cease to be held altogether. In the hill country, the markets appear to be unimportant—in fact, there is sometimes a small daily market in the place of the usual four-day one.

ARTS AND CRAFTS.—The most important native industry, apart from the production of food, is undoubtedly palm oil making. In each village may be seen the troughs in which the nuts are washed. After cutting them from the tree, the first operation is to boil them. They are then put into the troughs, which are filled up with water, and women trample the nuts until the oil floats on the surface, and the husk is separated from the kernel. The oil is then skimmed off and put into a pot; the next operation is to rinse the husks with water a second time, and the oil is again skimmed off. After a third rinsing and skimming the husks are removed from the water and put on one side for use in lighting; the kernels are put aside and cracked at a later period. The oil run from the husks is boiled and separated, the inferior part being reserved for lighting purposes.

Cotton is grown in some abundance in various parts of the country. It is frequently of good quality, and the thread made from it is strong, but as a rule the native is disposed to grow his cotton mixed up with other crops, such as beans, and the result is that the cotton crop suffers in quantity.

After the cotton fibre is removed from the plant, the first operation is to roll it on a block with an iron bar in order to remove the seed. It is then cleaned with a bow; to spin the cotton it is wound round the left arm or on a short stick held in the left hand. The end is made fast to a spindle consisting of a wooden rod passed through a disc made from a broken calabash. Drawing a portion of the cotton out, the woman gives a twist to the spindle, and in a very short time about a yard of thread is twisted. This is wound on the spindle and secured by a hitch, then a new length is made. When the spindle is full the thread may be wound off on to another spindle, or it may be wound upon a stretcher with movable pegs.

Two kinds of looms are in use, one used by women, which makes a comparatively short but broad piece of cloth; the other a man's loom, which produces a long and narrow fabric. The man's loom appears to be exceedingly rare among the Edo-speaking tribes, but the woman's loom is common in most places where European stores are not readily accessible.

The woman's loom is upright, and consists of two pillars with crossbars, round which run the woof threads, the shed is formed by a heddle rod wound with cotton for each piece of cloth; the warp thread is put through with a shuttle, and beaten down with a loom sword. The time taken to make a piece of cloth five feet long seems to be about three days. Coloured threads are employed to produce the patterns, for all of which native names exist. In some cases the dye stuffs are produced locally, from bark, seeds, or roots, in other cases they are purchased from Hausa or Yokuba traders.

As a rule the weaving, apart from the introduction of coloured threads, is quite straightforward, but occasionally an openwork pattern is produced by inserting loose threads and tying up five woof threads at intervals across the whole breadth of the cloth. This done, a warp thread is put in, five new threads are taken up to the right or the left of those taken up in the first instance, and another warp thread is put in. The number of threads between the insertions of the loose threads is forty or more, and when these have all been taken up, by moving the loose threads to the right or left an open chevron is produced. This pattern is repeated at intervals until the cloth is finished. As a rule cloth is made entirely of cotton threads, but in the hill country the inner bark of trees is occasionally used for the woof threads.

The man's loom is on an entirely different system ; heddle frames, worked with foot loops, produce the sheds, and much facilitate the making of the cloth. The warp thread is beaten home with a batten, and the cloth as it is finished is wound upon a revolving bar. The woof threads pass over a cross piece behind the heddles, and are made fast, some distance away, to a stone or other weight, by which the necessary tension is kept up.

Pottery is produced by exceedingly simple processes. The clay is, as a rule, purchased in the market. After being brought home, it is watered and worked with the feet till it is of the proper consistency. Then sausage-like rolls are prepared, and when a pot is to be made the potter seats herself, sometimes upon a piece of wood the size of a door, sometimes on the ground. As a base for the new pot the neck of an old one is taken. Clay is taken in the hand, formed into a lump, and thinned with the fingers until it can be placed in the neck, then a roll of clay is taken and added with the fingers to the base thus prepared ; and the pot is completed by the same method throughout. The neck and lip are formed by methods illustrated in an article published in "Man," July, 1910. After completion the outside of the pot is smoothed, and after being left to dry and decorated with ornamented marks it is baked in the fire, which is usually made of bark, plantain stalks, or like material, and is simply laid over the pot to be fired. The process of firing takes only about half an hour ; the pots appear to be durable, the price varies according to the size, from three pence upwards.

Numerous types of baskets are made in various parts of the country, the largest being some four feet high ; they are used for carrying food products home, or to the market, for storing such things as beans, and for fish traps. Basketwork frames are also used for drying tobacco.

Many kinds of mats are made, some highly decorated with

coloured patterns; they appear to be strong, and able to resist rough usage.

Except in Edo itself there appears to be little brasswork, though bracelets of brass, and in some parts broad brass collars, are not infrequent. Almost everywhere, however, blacksmiths are to be found, and with the rude materials at their disposal they appear to produce good work. At a few points in the hill country, more especially in the south centre of the Kaba province, smelting furnaces are found. Elsewhere iron is acquired from European sources. Hoes appear to be the objects most commonly produced, and the ordinary market price is ninepence. The blacksmith's forge is also much used for the repair of cutlasses and knives. Occasionally other objects, such as lamps and magical instruments, are produced.

SECTION II.

RELIGION AND MAGIC.

RELIGION.—Religion appears to play a considerable part in the lives and thoughts of the Edo-speaking people. There is no house but has its household shrine and household worship, both of the so-called Ebǫ and of the ancestors. Each village or each quarter has its seasonal celebrations, and over all is a supreme deity, commonly called Osa or Osalobula. Osa receives no regular sacrifice in many cases, but he is far from being the ordinary type of the otiose creator, remote from mankind and indifferent to them, not only does he figure largely in their folk tales, but his name is constantly upon their lips, and his emblem, a long pole with white cloth on it, is to be seen in nearly every village. He is regarded as the creator of the world, and a myth is told in which Osanowa, or Osa of the house, has an evil counterpart, Osanoha, or Osa of the bush. Osanowa created man ; Osanoha created animals. Osanoha also made a sickness house, in which were all diseases. When men and women came near this house, on their way from heaven to earth, rain fell and they entered it to escape from it. In this way sickness came to the earth, and Osanoha being the creator of animals, man became their enemy, and so, whenever he sees an animal, he kills it. Another version of this story says that Osanowa and Osanoha agreed to reckon up their riches, and the children of Osanoha were more than the children of Osanowa. Hence they are enemies.

In answer to the direct question, a native will probably say that he does not know where Osa is, and in fact this answer, " I do not know," is the one that is most commonly given when questions are put about the future life. If, however, in the place of putting questions, the enquirer encourages natives to tell him their folk tales, he will find that Osa, together with subordinate members of the pantheon, are in Elimi (heaven), whither go also dead people and the sacrifices which are offered to them.

Subordinate to Osa are a number of Ebǫ, such as Ake, Ochwaie, and others. Tradition says that these Ebǫ were originally followers of King Ewale, and that after following him for a great number of years they perished in a fire.

Egwaibo, or temples, sacred to these Ebǫ, are found in various places in the Edo country. Annually sacrifices are offered at the various centres, and people come from far and near to take part in the celebration. Sacrifices are made and dances performed, and in certain cases there is a custom of stopping the road or of exacting contributions from passers-by.

In addition to these Ebǫ there are various objects in use among the Edo which they call Uxumu, or medicine. These are magical implements for the protection of person or property. There is little or no idea of personality attached to them, but sacrifices may be offered to them in exactly the same way as to the more personal Ebǫ. As we proceed north, however, from Edo we notice a curious change. In Edo itself the Ebǫ are numerous; tradition says that there are two hundred and one, but this is simply taken to represent an indefinite number, for we find this number of two hundred and one recurring in the folk tales.

When we leave Edo, some of these Ebǫ who have clearly been derived from the Yoruba, disappear altogether, others appear to become depersonalised. They fall in the scale and take their places beside the medicine, and though they receive sacrifice, their personal character has become at least obscure, if it has not vanished altogether. This tendency seems to reach its highest point in Okpe, where I noticed a curious uncertainty about Osa, who is otherwise the one persistent figure in the pantheon. One or two of my informants said that Osa looked like a cloud. This does not of course necessarily mean more than that he was originally a sky-god, but the general impression which I gathered there was that much had been forgotten, and that on the whole medicine was becoming more important, and the personal deity less important. It must not be forgotten in this connection that over a great part of the area images of deities are non-existent. For example, in Okpe, Osa is represented by a tree with a white cloth round it. The little figure of Esu, the mischievous deity, is found outside the houses, but he is undoubtedly an importation from the Yoruba country. Elsewhere Osa is frequently represented by a pot. Now pots and calabashes suspended from the roof, or resting on trees in the courtyard, are everywhere recognised as medicine, whose function is to keep people alive; which is in the long run, the object of nearly every ceremony and every cult. Perhaps, therefore, we may recognise a double current of change; the medicine rites have taken over some of the features of the more personal cults, such as sacrifice; and conversely, the impersonal medicine rites, by the analogy of their representatives to the representatives of the Ebọ, have led to loss of personality in what were originally deities.

The question is, however, far from simple. It is complicated in the first case by an apparent forgetfulness of much which must have been known before, and by the evident neglect of cults which formerly flourished, of which the broken down state of the building dedicated to these cults is conclusive evidence. On the other hand, it must be considered that when questions are put to the old men and to the young, the latter are always far less well informed, though they are often more ready to communicate what they know to the enquirer. Where it was possible to obtain information from a priest or a doctor, the ignorance to which I have alluded was much less pronounced, and the depersonalisation was far less noticeable.

As to the real beliefs it is impossible to be very definite. The ordinary man will tell you that the ebọ is in the stones laid down, before his shrine, or, more rarely, identify him with the image, where one exists in the Edo country. The esoteric lore is that the ebọ uses images and stones as his tools, and descends from climi to partake of the sacrifice; this at any rate makes it clear that among the better informed there is no belief in a multitude of local ebọ bearing the same name, which seems to be the view of the masses.

The European observer is prone to attribute a spiritual theory of divinities to the people of lower grades of culture. An enquirer without prepossessions would have little or no ground for making any such assumption with regard to the Edo-speaking peoples. Stories are told of Osa which attribute to him a body like that of man; the Ogiuwu seem to be possessed of a human body; the general conception of the ehi attributes to it substance, and there is nothing to suggest that climi is the abode of spirits. True, there are suggestions that the ebọ are invisible except to priests, and that the dead can only be seen by those who wash their faces with medicine; but there is a very definite belief that the dead carry their funeral offerings with them, and invisibility, though not incorporeality, is asserted of witches also.

The general impression left on the mind is that if we are face to face with animism, it is animism of a very vague kind, mingled with much that is irreconcilable with purely spiritual theory.

The familiar household ebọ does not seem to excite apprehension in the mind of the native; he lives in daily intercourse, as it were, with his deity, and does not fear to draw supernatural penalities upon himself by too great boldness; it must be remembered that it is rare for any but great chiefs to have a priest to attend to the household cult.

In the case of the greater ebọ, however, like Oxwaie, who have an egwaibo, there is a reluctance to enter the shrine in which are deposited the stones and other emblems of the deity. Not until the presence of the priest gives him a sense of security will the ordinary man enter such a hut; a man of a different tribe will often display no reluctance whatever, for reverence goes hand in hand with belief.

The same feeling was manifested with regard to ceremonial dresses. They could not be carried by men of the same village, nor yet be taken near the houses: men from a neighbouring village, who must have been aware of the character of the loads, displayed no reluctance to carry them, and one native, who was scrupulous in his own country, entered without fear the house in which the dresses were kept.

Another instructive incident happened at the same place. On the square in front of the rest-house is a small hut, open at both ends, which contains a drum used only in certain festivals. There is a house close to one end of the hut, and women going to and fro from this house, as well as those crossing the square, can readily cast a glance at the treasure it contains.

The chief was informed that a photograph of the drum was to be taken ; but, before it could be brought out, all doors had to be shut, and women were warned to keep their distance by deafening cries of "Hoi."

Generally speaking there is much more reluctance to let women hear or see anything of men's rites than anything which can be properly described as reverence. In one village, when the sweepings of the Egwaibo were brought out, women were warned by the piercing notes of the Oko to keep away ; yet some of the shrines were cleaned by women : women have to do the rubbing of the Ovia house, from which they are ordinarily excluded ; and a woman in a purificatory ceremony carried the uxure of Ake and entered by the elimi gate.

At Otua the initiants are required to sleep away from home for a night before the eliminya celebrations; but in the case of the Ovia rites the seclusion is for a whole month, during which all males are enjoined to practise continence. So far is the dread of female onlookers carried, that they are warned to keep their distance when nothing more elaborate or dangerous than materials for the manufacture of the Ovia hats are being transported through the village. Singularly enough the dresses of some are at the conclusion of the ceremonies hung upon posts outside the precincts, and actually bordering the path to the village, so that women not only see but, it may be, touch them.

Occasionally a very definite manifestation of dread of the supernatural came under observation. In all quarters of one village they have an ebọ called Obazu covered with a cloth, to lift which even in the absence of onlookers might have serious consequences; the sight of Obazu was believed to cause death.

Again, in one case there was some difficulty in getting a record of the Ovia songs, owing to the fear of the men that women might hear them; yet these very songs had been sung in the presence of the women a few nights previously.

In connection with religious awe must be mentioned the rites connected with the hunting of big game and the similar observances imposed upon some or all the mourners at a funeral. These customs are usually explained as due to the fear of the spirit of the dead animal or man, and there is this to be said for the view in the case of burial rites, that there is a well-marked rite of dismissing the dead to his own place, which is done on the last day of the burial rites. However, the mourning customs are practised later than this, but it may be that they are of earlier origin, and that the dismissal of the dead has been superposed upon them, and indeed it is by no means universal.

Seclusion at birth is very rare; in fact, it seems to prevail only at Fuga and in one place in the Sobo country. Seclusion during menstruation is practised to a limited extent, and apparently only by a woman living in her husband's house, although of course she has her own room there in the oderie, if she is the wife of a big chief.

Sacrifice appears to be everywhere an offering of food or drink required by the bodily needs of the recipient. It is definitely stated that the dead take their funeral offerings to climi, and that they are there shared among the members of the family. In Otua sacrifice was described as payment for work, and the indispensable alligator pepper as a stimulant to ensure the speedy action of the recipient. (In this connection may be noted an Ikhe custom of lighting a fire under medicine against sickness to make it " strong.")

Occasionally sacrificial meats must be wholly consumed, and there is usually provision to secure that all in a village receive their share. The washing of the hands during the rite is the only indication of anything like ceremonial purity in the sacrificer. The victims are not subjected to any preparation, but precautions are taken to prevent them from uttering cries while they are being slaughtered.

Ritual.—As an example of the cults of the Ebọ, we may take the worship of Ake at Idumowina, a village of about two hundred inhabitants some seven miles north of Edo.

There is a large Egwaibo here, which is, however, of comparatively recent origin, probably not more than fifty years old. It is decorated with a large number of images comprising Osa, Olokun, Ogun, and other Ebọ, together with a large number of subsidiary figures. Ake is worshipped here annually in April for about fourteen days.

In addition to the Egwaibo there are a number of smaller shrines, at all of which sacrifices are offered during the main ceremony. The first act in preparation for the coming ceremony was for the priest to make a circuit of all the shrines and ask a blessing. On the following day the minor shrines were cleaned by the women and the Egwaibo was cleaned and decorated by the men, women being warned to keep out of the way when the rubbish was being carried off. These preparations finished, the Egwaibo was opened, and men and women danced; offerings of kola were made, and the images were painted. In the evening dancing began in the Egwaibo, preceded by a sacrifice in the ogwedion or shrine of the ancestors of the village. On the evening of the following day sacrifices were offered, and the killing of a goat to Osa may be taken as a typical one. The goat was brought before the shrine of Osa, and the priest took hold of the end of the rope. Then he rang his bell and offered prayer, during which those present ejaculated " I s e." Then a bowl of chalk was brought, with which marks were made by the priest in front of the shrine, the goat being held by a boy while he did so. Kola was offered to Osa and his wife. Then the goat's legs were held and the rope removed : the mouth of the goat was tightly held to prevent it uttering a sound, and a small cut was made behind its ear. The blood from this was poured out into a bowl before the shrine of Osa; all those who were present shouted "gale." Then the throat was cut completely through and blood smeared on the back of the priest; finally the head was cut clean off, blood from it was rubbed on the shrine, and the head itself was laid on the shrine; blood was next poured from the bowl upon the shrine and the head taken out ; a piece of skin was then cut from the left-hand side of the neck, prayer was offered, and the skin was fixed to the beam above the shrine. Finally the priest stood in front of the shrine with the knife and made three strokes vertically, calling each time " Osalobwa." Sacrifices were offered to Ogun, Olokun, Ake, and the Idiọñ of the priest. These finished, the priest proceeded to a shrine of Ake in a private house and offered further sacrifice there. Then the whole company wended its way to the shrine of Akenilo, distant half a mile from the village.

In connection with the cult of Ake may be mentioned a method of discovering stolen goods, called aiabobewimi, that is, taking the ebọ to call out, " Who took my goods ? " This is forbidden by the Government, but there are numerous opportunities of seeing the rite in operation. A dish is taken in which are placed a small bowl with cowries on it and other emblems of Ake. This is put upon the head of a girl ; the loser of the property accompanies her with a bell and rings it, singing, " The one who took my fowl, if he does not bring it back, may the Ebọ kill him."

Another important Ebọ is known as Olokun, who is a sea

or river god, worshipped also in the Sobo country. The cult of Olokun seems to be confined to the women, and in the Sobo country women go to a camp of Olokun in the same way that men go to the camp of Ovia. The emblems of Olokun are usually pots containing water, pieces of chalk, peeled rods, and white cloth.

Outside the doors of houses in the kingdom of Edo, the Ora country, parts of Northern Nigeria, and the kingdom of Agbede, may be seen a figure in mud or, sometimes, a thorny piece of wood. This is the image of the mischievous Esu, who is said to have come from beyond Ilorin. The image of Esu is set up in the gate to keep him out of the house, for if he comes in man and wife fight and fire breaks out. According to the folk tales, Esu is the doorkeeper of Elimi.

Another important Ebọ is Oxwaie, worshipped especially at Eviakoi and Ulola. His rites do not differ in any important particular to those of Ake. When Oxwaie comes out at these places no one may go on that day to Enyai market. People call this ugbodeniái, that is, shutting the road of Enyai.

Another Ebọ is known as Osun. He is especially connected with the native doctors, and as a protective deity he is usually found in the village gate. His emblem is the so called osunematọñ, a piece of iron planted in the ground with various emblems. Osun is found as a subsidiary shrine in connection with the shrines of Ake, Ochwaie, and other Ebọ.

Ogun, the blacksmith, is represented by an iron knife or image of iron. He is worshipped by men generally, but especially by blacksmiths. But if there is no son in a family, women too may sacrifice to him.

If a man falls sick without a cause he would sometimes sacrifice to Alucre, which means literally "others." It is not uncommon to see a small circle in front of a house with offerings of kola, etc., in it. This is an offering to Aluere.

Women have various objects which they worship, in the first place Obiame, the mother of all mankind, as her name indicates. In addition they frequently sacrifice also to a shrine called Omeiho, represented by a pile of small ant hills beneath a tree outside a village.

Another cult of some interest is that of Akobie, a child's deity, represented by a human figure on the wall of a house. Inside the house itself are various shrines, such as the shrine of the hand, the shrine of mother, and the shrine of father. The two latter will be noticed in connection with the cult of ancestors.

Mention may be made of some of the " medicines " which are found in the houses ; a small mound may sometimes be seen in the centre of the floor with four sticks round it, or the skull of a goat or other animal may be let into the floor and surrounded with cowries. Sacrifice is offered to these "medicines" in precisely the same way as to a personal deity. Other " medicines " are portable ; one is known as Ohumewele. In the morning, before saluting anyone, the owner wets his finger with saliva, draws it over the " medicine " and then down his forehead, saying, " May every man, woman, and child do good to me."

Magic.—It is unnecessary to describe in detail the Ebǫ of all the various tribes of the Edo-speaking peoples. But something may be said with regard to their magical implements and the practice of magic generally. As a rule it was exceedingly difficult to obtain details of the manufacture of " medicine," for they were regarded as trade secrets, and no doctor was in the least disposed to reveal them. At Otua, however, I succeeded in winning the confidence of a native doctor ; from his account it appears that the method of making " medicine " is fairly uniform.

If " medicine " is to be made from a certain piece of wood it is ground up, mixed with alligator pepper and other products, and the doctor repeats words to the effect that once it was a tree in the bush and now it is " medicine." I obtained precisely the same account of the making of " medicine " at Sabongida, and there can be no doubt that this is the essential feature of the ceremony.

In connection with magic, mention may also be made of witchcraft, ceremonies of purification, and other rites. The belief in witches appears to be almost universal, and in more than one place complaints were made to me that since the white man has forbidden the use of the sass wood ordeal the number of witches is greatly on the increase. There can be no doubt that the mortality by witch trials must have been enormous formerly; an epidemic broke out at Fuga a few months before I got there, and it is estimated that at least eighty people lost their lives before it was suppressed. Witches are believed to meet at night in precisely the same way as European folk belief supposes them to come together. They fly through the air invisibly, and only a doctor can see them. By means of "medicines" a doctor would be able to cause them to fall to the ground, and I have been assured by more than one man that he has been present when a witch has been brought to the ground in this way.

Witches are everywhere known and dreaded, and in many parts of the country may be seen along the roads fragments of calabashes, with cowries or food ; these have been offered to the witches. In many places the native doctors must make considerable sums by their intervention to protect sick people against the witches. It is commonly supposed that sickness is due to the malevolence of some human being, and that ordinary skill is insufficient to restore the sufferer to health. If a native doctor is consulted, he informs the sick man that his illness is due to the witches, and that they demand an offering. It is believed that this offering must be made through a native doctor, who alone can converse in safety with the witches. The offering is made at night, and the edible part of it is the perquisite of the doctor. A relative of the sick man is often concealed in the neighbourhood of the place where the offering is made, in order that he may recognise the witch.

If a man falls sick he will go to the diviner and enquire what is the cause of his sickness. He may be told to offer a sacrifice to his father, or more probably to the witches. Any man who is troubled by a witch sends for a doctor, who goes at night to the road of the bush and talks to the witches, whom he can recognise when he sees them if he puts " medicine " on his face. He summons them by blowing an ivory horn, and begs them to leave the man alone. If they are not holding the man tight, as the native saying is, they will ask for a goat; the witch asks the doctor if he is alone, or if a brother or a father of the sick man is in hiding; but the doctor assures the witch that there is no one there; and they come to take their sacrifice.

Witches come in human form, but they have mouths like birds, and feathers on their bodies. Another account says that they have birds in their stomachs, and at dark these birds come out and fly wherever they wish. The body of the witch remains at home apparently asleep, but it is impossible to arouse it. If the doctor could catch the bird, it would be possible to kill the witch, but to attack the body is useless, for the gun would miss fire.

A witch is said to possess his power from birth, and the power which they possess is regarded by the natives as qualitatively identical with that of the native doctor. The witch is often regarded as more powerful, and the doctor is supposed to protect himself against them by means of " medicine."

It is said in some places that if a witch comes to attack a doctor, the latter will be waked by his " medicine."

Sacrifice.—Human sacrifices were common in Edo itself before European rule, but they do not appear to have been practised elsewhere.

Among the sacrifices were those to the sun, the rain, and the year. These victims were crucified on trees within the city. Another custom enjoined that once a year a lame man should be dragged around the city, and then as far as a place on the Enyai road, called Adaneha. This was probably a ceremony of purification.

Purificatory ceremonies play a considerable part in the life of the people, and some account of a typical one may be given here. If a man feels unwell, he will make circular marks on the ground either with his feet or with chalk. An eggshell is then spiked on a short piece of stick, and the person who is performing the ceremony stands in each circle in turn, rotates, points the eggshell to the sun, blows along the stick, and repeats words implying that any evil which is in this body must leave it.

Another form of purification requires one or two persons to operate in addition to the suppliant. Seven circles of cowries are made, and the penitent is led along these and his or her body brushed with leaves or a chicken, which is then thrown away.

General purifications are also known. At Gwaton a diviner will sometimes order isusu to be driven out. All take their cutlasses and run about the town. Then they get a stick, tie leaves at the top, roast and tie on a head of corn, and put a bush buck's head on the top. With this in their hands a procession goes round all the houses, and the stick with the emblems is waved over the heads of the people, songs being sung at the same time to the effect that the sickness is to go away.

In another form of purification a chicken or small animal is passed round the head and thrown through the legs. The chicken is then transfixed on the midrib of a palm leaf, which is planted upright at cross roads or where a path branches from the main road.

As may be imagined from the fact that the people depend almost entirely upon agriculture for their food, there are various ceremonies which have for their object the welfare of the crops. In Edo during the king's time a small plot of ground called the King's Farm was cultivated on the Sapoba road by a slave who was known as the " fowl of the farm." Omens were drawn from the growth of the yams planted there, and the produce eventually brought to the king.

The ordinary man sets up an ebo called utu on his farm which is in many cases a specially large yam heap. On this are put down the cutlasses and hoes, together with a calabash of palm wine. A sacrifice, often of a snail, is offered, and the owner of the farm calls upon the yams to come and eat, together with all the other ebǫ upon the farm.

In addition to this, in the kingdom of Edo, on each farm road may be seen three sticks planted upright in the ground. These are called idiogbo and represent the first people who ever made farms along that road. A sacrifice is offered to them in the same way as to other ancestors.

In some places the women have a similar ebǫ, called ugiame or igiame, which represents the first women who ever went to cultivate a farm in its second year.

Cults of Ancestors.—In addition to the cults of Osa and the Ebǫ, the cult of ancestors plays an important part in the life of the Edo-speaking peoples.

While the king was still in Benin City human victims were offered to the ancestors by important chiefs. At the present day cows, or more often goats, are the victim. Celebrations take place, apparently on the anniversary of the death of a man, for years after, and processions march round the town in precisely the same way as for the funeral. These rites, however, appear to be peculiar to Edo itself; poor people and inhabitants of the villages content themselves with the annual sacrifice to the dead man.

The ancestors of a man are represented by the so-called nohure. These are long wooden staves with decorative carving, the top of which is often shaped like a hand. A few inches below the top the staff is hollow, and a piece of wood left inside rattles when the nohure is beaten on the ground at a sacrifice. In addition to the uchure, the ancestors of chiefs are represented by uhumilau, heads of bronze or wood, on which rested formerly the ivory tusks, which were also regarded as representing the deceased ancestors.

The customs with regard to the sacrifice offered annually to the ancestors differ from tribe to tribe. In some cases sacrifices are offered by all the sons, in others only by the head son. Daughters sometimes sacrifice for themselves, sometimes their husbands sacrifice for them, and sometimes they are represented by their brothers.

Secret Societies.—Under this head may be noticed not only societies of which the rites are kept secret from women, but also the masked figures which appear at certain times of the year. In the walls of the houses in the kingdom of Edo may be observed a small niche, or an altar, always on the outside of the wall. Many of these contain a piece of wood or stone, cowries and chalk, and as a rule they are shrines of Ovia.

The story told to account for the origin of the society is that Ovia was a woman, the wife of a certain king who was loved by her husband and hated by other women. By a trick they caused her husband to quarrel with her, and she turned into water. She instituted a society which bears her name, and said that women must not know the secrets nor enter the camp. Ovia therefore is worshipped by men, and women only enter the camp once or twice in each year to clean the shrine and to sing the accompaniments to the ritual dance.

There appears to be some confusion in the story, for when one of the society goes in procession round the village to bless the people, as representative of Ovia, he is always addressed as Erhame, my father. On the other hand, the principal mask of the Ovia society is known as the mother mask.

The Ovia society is completely harmless. I watched the ceremonies for a whole month, and was permitted to record texts and vocabularies in the secret language, which is syntactically the same as the ordinary language, with words drawn from Yoruba, Ishan, and other neighbouring languages.

As a rule, all the males in any village in which it is found belong to the society. At the beginning of the dry season they go to the camp of Ovia, a little distance from the village, and sleep there for the whole of one month. They appear in the village sometimes at night, sometimes in the day, and on some of these occasions ceremonial dress, of which the most prominent feature is a large hat decorated with parrot feathers, is worn by all the members. As a rule women are excluded from the camp, and only visit it for one ceremonial dance. On some of the occasions when the sons of Ovia visit the village, the women are not permitted to come out of the house; on other occasions they march round the village and act as the chorus.

The precise meaning of the Ovia ceremonies cannot be discovered at the present day, but the function ascribed to them by the natives is that of keeping people alive. It is possible that in the first instance they were connected with agriculture.

Corresponding to the Ovia society in the Edo country are societies for the youths and small boys; these do not call for any further notice.

In the Ora country, Okpe, Otna, and parts of Northern Nigeria, the ceremonies connected with the initiation of young men into their otu resemble in some degree the rites of a secret society. At Otua the young men are secluded for a time and dress up with masks and other ceremonial dresses, with which they parade the town and dance, sometimes for some weeks. Elsewhere the ritual is less elaborate, and the ceremony may be whittled down to the wearing of good clothes, eating, and drinking.

In the Edo country, and occasionally elsewhere, masked figures appear at certain times of the year.

As an example may be mentioned Igodo, seven men who appeared at Gwaton. They danced round the town and all the women were shut up in the houses from 7 p.m. onwards. When they returned at daybreak women might see them, and they continued the dance till 6 p.m., when a goat was sacrificed of which no woman might eat. The object of the ceremony was probably purificatory.

Soul.—Beliefs about the soul appear to be on the whole much vaguer than one would imagine from reading works on the subject of animism.

The people of Edo say that every man has e hi, which comes to him at birth and goes to Elimi when he dies.

There is also a belief in a second ehi, called ehinoha, or bush ehi: ehinoha, however, does not correspond precisely with the " bush soul " of Calabar, though I was told that occasionally an injury to ehinoha would result in an injury in the health of the man. A more common view seems to be that ehinoha is a sort of evil genius, which leads a man to do evil.

It is said by some to live on the back of the neck, others say that it is a servant to the real ehi. Others again that it corresponds to ere.[1] Others again that ehinoha is a man's shadow in Osa's house in Elimi. At Sabongida I found the most definite beliefs with regard to the ehi; but Sabongida is the seat of a native mission, and I am disposed to think that the genuine native belief has been considerably influenced in this way.

I frequently put the question, "Do you ever see dead people after they are dead ? " And from older informants, the almost invariable answer was " No." When, however, I questioned the younger generation, I found that stories of ghosts and apparitions at the moment of death were as common in West Africa as they are in Europe.

Burial.—The burial customs of the Edo-speaking peoples depend for their character very largely upon whether the deceased has left children or not. In a certain number of cases childless people may be buried by brothers or sisters with the same ceremonies as those who have left descendants, and this whether they are men or women. But, as a rule, the heirless man or woman receives treatment little or no better than the child who is simply thrown into the bush. Other differences depend upon the rank or wealth of the deceased, for a rich man can afford to prolong the burial ceremonies where a poor man is compelled to bring them to an end quickly. In connection with marriage ceremonies, mention will be made of the awaigbe,[2] and the ceremonies with regard to this naturally vary from family to family. The grave was formerly dug in the room known as the " father's

---

[1] See p. 32.   [2] See p. 61.

room," and where Government regulations are unknown or can be disregarded, this is still the recognised custom, except in the areas where burial in the bush is the prescribed rite.

A distinguishing feature of the funeral rites in Edo itself is the use of the Otǫñ or burial shrine, an object covered with Manchester cloth and tinsel. In some families a figurine is used in its place, and there can be little doubt that the original meaning of the custom was that the Otǫñ represented the dead man.

A generalised account of the burial ceremonies may be given. The first act is to wash the body and place it, usually wrapped in white cloth, upon the bed. A goat or a fowl is sacrificed close to this bed to the feet of the dead body, and the reason given for this sacrifice is that it makes the dead person strong to go to heaven. The grave is dug either by relatives of the deceased or, in the villages, by the Igele.

During the burial rites traditional burial songs are sung. The burial is attended sometimes by the family of the deceased only, sometimes by the wives also. After the grave is filled in a sacrifice is sometimes offered upon it, and the gravediggers purify themselves with water or with a chicken.

Sacrifices go on night and morning for a varying number of days, and where the awaigbe is used, the final act is to purify with afo. On the last night of the burial ceremonies, which are of course prolonged for some time after the body has been put in the grave, and may, if the family is a poor one, be postponed for years after the actual burial, a member of the family dresses up to represent the dead man, whose seat he occupies.

An important point to be noted in connection with the burial ceremonies is that the sons-in-law of the dead man have to bring contributions of cloth, yams, cocoanuts, and other objects, together with one goat.

If a question arises as to whether a daughter has been actually married to a certain man or not, evidence for or against the alleged marriage may be gained by enquiring whether, if her father is dead, the supposed husband brought contributions to the funeral expenses.

In Ijeba the king has a special form of burial appropriated to himself. No one laments for him until after the new king has been chosen, and if his sons contravene this regulation they may be fined £5. On the day on which death takes place seven cows are killed in the king's house, then two low walls are made and sticks are put across. On these are placed a mat, and on the mat the body of the king. Then the walls are built higher and the top is roofed over.

Various sacrifices are offered, and as soon as the new king has been chosen, the walls of the temporary tomb are opened, and the body of the dead king is put upon a bed. The body remains nine days in the house, and the corpse is carried out by the ceremonial gate. In the street a sacrifice is offered to the right hand, and the king's widows are brought to the spot. Each woman covers her face with a cloth and swears to hand over all the late king's property; they then return to the house. After this the body is carried to the grave and buried by the Otu in the quarter of Iviogulu. There are four different places of interment here, one for the king, and one each for big chiefs, small chiefs, and women chiefs. Common people are buried on the road to Iviogulu.

Suicides are buried in the same way as other people, but if a member of the royal family commits suicide the king may punish him by having his body exposed. It is believed that unburied people take nothing to heaven with them; consequently, when such a man reaches heaven there is nothing to show that he is of royal blood.

If a man is killed by a crocodile, or if his body is for some reason irrecoverable, a palm leaf is gathered and carried with a pot to the road by which the dead man left the town. A son or daughter calls the dead man's name and touches the ground with the leaf, calling on the dead man to come home. Then the leaf and the pot are taken home and put upon the bed; they receive sacrifices and are buried in the usual way.

In the Uzaitui country, when a man dies, they wash the

body, wrap it in a cloth and mat, and lean it against the wall inside the room. A fire is then made at the foot of a mound of earth, just below the corpse, and it is kept burning until sufficient money is collected to bury the dead man : this usually occupies about four days. On the morning of the day of the funeral the head son buys a big goat, and the head of the compound kills it in the street before the house. The meat is shared between the head of the compound and the three oldest men, and the bearers of the body walk through the goat's blood. When the body is being carried to the place of burial in the bush, it is placed, in the case of an old man, in a shallow trunk hollowed out like a canoe, which is carried away and used again. In the case of young people a framework or flat bier of bamboo is used, and this is placed upon the small mound which marks the grave. On the way to the grave cowries are thrown on the road : daughters may go to the grave, but no other females. After the grave is filled in all return to the house of the head of the compound, who gives water to the bearers, with which they wash their hands. It is forbidden to bury anyone during the last two months of the wet season, and if anyone dies the body is put in the bush, and they wait till the period of tabu is over.

At Uzia, in the kingdom of Agbede, the body is washed and dressed in a white loin cloth, then a leaf mat is put round it, and a big white cover cloth ; it is the duty of each son to bring a cloth and a mat, and the surplus cloth is divided when the burial ceremonies are over. After the corpse has been buried comes the so-called second burial. The married daughters bring a goat, cowries, a small cloth, and three small sticks of bamboo. The bamboo is covered with cloth and put upon the grave, it is then called the corpse. A goat is bought by the sons and sacrificed to the bamboo, and all goats belonging to the sons and daughters are sent to be killed. The same night two men bring the bamboos to the spot where the goats have been killed, and when all are asleep they take the sticks away and dispose of them.

In the Ibie country, Northern Nigeria, the son of a dead man announces his death to the big men of the town, and brings a long drum, which he beats to announce it to other people. The women too have their own drum, and summon the old women. During the burial ceremonies a masked man, called Elo, carries a thin stick and walks through the town, driving away small boys and girls, who say that the dead man has come out.

After the burial they play igbedo; all the men of the town take their guns, and act like men who go to war. An image is made with cloth and sticks and put on the roof of the house. Two men take the figure on their shoulders and they march round the town to the sound of the drum. After a dance the body (cloth) is taken to pieces and the sticks are thrown away. Five days after the customs are finished mourners wash and put black and white thread on their wrists.

At Soso the grave is dug in the house, sometimes in the middle of the room, in the case of a big man, otherwise outside the door of the room. Before the burial takes place the man's cap, gown, and other garments are taken, and a figure made out of them with the help of three sticks. This figure is called Mamači, and is put on the roof. If it is a woman who has died, they take a calabash which she used for trading and cover it with red cloth. If she has left a daughter-in-law, the daughter-in-law takes the calabash and dances round the town.

In the Sobo country, as in Northern Nigeria, objects are sometimes taken to represent the dead man. At Ovu the body is buried in the house, and a kid is sacrificed on the grave. When the "second burial" takes place a canoe-shaped object about two feet high and two feet long is carved by the people of the town, and covered while it is still in the bush with two pieces of white cloth. This canoe is carried home by two members of the family, and the people of the town dance and throw cowries over it. After sacrifices have been offered a second grave is dug by the sons and sons-in-law in the same room as the original grave, and the canoe is put into it. That this canoe represents the body is sufficiently obvious, but if further proof were required, it would be supplied by the fact that if the body cannot be recovered two canoes are buried.

Mourning.—Mourning customs comprise, firstly, the washing of the hands, or of hands and feet, or of the whole body, by the gravediggers and bearers; and, secondly, washing of the whole body by members of the family. In addition to this, members of the family have to shave their heads, and various fashions are prescribed according to the relationship in which they stand to the dead man. At Fuga, for example, the right side is shaved for the father, the left for the mother, and the whole head if both die. If the parents are dead the whole head is shaved for a brother or for a sister; otherwise only the middle. If a boy dies whose father's father is still alive, the father of the deceased shaves only the middle of his head. A wife shaves the whole of her head, but leaves patches over her right and left ears if her father and mother are alive. Sometimes only the head wife shaves.

An **Amoiya** wife is sometimes forbidden to shave for her father; for her husband, she shaves as a rule at the end of three months, because that is the interval which is allowed to elapse before the property is divided.

An **Isomi** wife, on the other hand, who leaves the family at once, shaves her head at once.

In certain places restrictions are placed upon the widows. At **Gwaton**, for example, she must sleep upon the floor, holding a small broom in her hand; she may not cook nor do any household work for seven days; she may not wash for seven days, and after that, she has to perform her ablutions in the road about an hour after sunset.

In the kingdom of **Edo** a widow sometimes puts up two pieces of wood with a cross piece by the side of the road, and hangs a piece of cloth over them. In some places, however, this custom is carried out by the gravediggers.

At Ibilo. in Northern Nigeria, a widow shaves and puts her hair upon the grave. After this she puts white thread on her neck, which must remain there till it falls off. She is not, however, forbidden to take a husband while the thread is still on her neck.

SECTION III.

MARRIAGE AND BIRTH.

MARRIAGE.—Among the Edo-speaking people we find, broadly speaking, two forms of marriage; in the first (termed in these pages amoiya) the woman becomes the property of the husband; at his death she passes to his heirs, and her children succeed him; this is the normal form in the southern part of the area; in the northern part of the area, so far from the wife being the property of the husband, she is at liberty to leave him at any time if the bride price is repaid, and even this is not essential if she has borne him a child (isomi marriage).

Almost invariably the suitor begins to pay the bride price while the girl is extremely young; he may ask for her hand when she is only a few days old, but it seldom happens that she is handed over to him before she is marriageable.

The widow as a rule passes to the heirs of the dead man but in certain cases she is free to marry if she has borne children. In Edo itself there are two forms of marriage which however only differ according to the age of the girl. If she is quite small the suitor approaches her father and when he gives his consent, brings him a piece of cloth, yams, a goat, or some other small present. A family council is then summoned by the girl's father and they meet at his house. The suitor is introduced to the family, and, if they approve of him, he sends them a present of gin. In theory, at any rate, the father is obliged to pay attention to the views of his elder brother, but whether the elder brother has an absolute veto is a point at which evidence is contradictory.

Until the girl is of marriageable age various payments and services are required of the suitor, details of which will be given below.

When she reaches puberty the father arranges for her body marks to be made, and the suitor contributes food. This done the suitor is entitled to ask the father to give him his wife. At the same time he sends a present of two hundred cocoanuts, two hundred kola, five demijohns of palm wine, and a certain number of cowries. This is shared out by the father among the family, and a second present may then be asked for.

When the girl is taken to her husband the father summons members of his family to act as conductors. They lead the girl to her husband in the evening, and receive presents from him. An essential feature of the reception of the girl is the washing of her hands. The husband puts seven hundred cowries, four kola, and a bottle of gin on each of two plates, and brings water in a basin. A member of the girl's family carries the basin and washes the girl's hands, then the husband brings a cloth and wipes them. The towel and the seven hundred cowries go to the girl, and her conductors receive the other plate.

This constitutes the whole ceremony of marriage. It is difficult to say which part, if any, is regarded as essential— payment of the bride price is undoubtedly the important feature; and if the bride price has never been paid, it seems that the father can reclaim his daughter and her children at any time. How far the omission of any of the other factors would affect the validity of the marriage is a point I was never able to clear up.

It has been mentioned above that there is a second form of marriage. In this case the girl is already adult, and has no suitor who is paying bride price for her. A man approaches the girl directly and enquires if she has a husband. If she says that she has not, he goes to her father and asks for her hand. The next day he goes again and takes some friends to help him. Then if her father is disposed to accept him, the suitor brings beads worth seventy shillings or so, and in the pre-European days a boy slave. Then he is at liberty to fetch the girl.

The customs as to payment seem to vary considerably in different parts of the old kingdom of Edo. The responsibility of the family is also more pronounced in Edo itself than in the villages, at any rate at the present day; for it is by no means uncommon to find people in the villages who cannot even say who is the head of their house, and it is quite certain that unless the elder brother resides in the village he is seldom consulted.

At Ugo on the eastern border of the Edo country, no bride price is paid in money, though the usual payments of kola, cocoanuts, and yams are made.

At Eviakoi the customs are again somewhat different. A suitor begs for a girl as soon as she is born. If the father and mother accept him he takes firewood to the mother and goes to salute her every day for seven days. On the seventh day he takes four kola, palm wine, and cocoanuts to the father, who has to send for the elders of the town. The headman breaks the kola and calls on the others to eat it, and then two doctors divine whether the girl shall be betrothed. If the answer is favourable, the suitor has from this time on to take a certain number of yams, a leg of duiker, four kola, and a calabash of palm wine for the father, and for the mother seven yams, a calabash of oil, and a leg of duiker; these contributions are payable twice a year, but similar presents may be brought or demanded at other times. Here and elsewhere the suitor is called upon to collect a number of hands to help his prospective father-in-law in his farm work. When the girl is marked the suitor goes to salute her and sends her two loads of fufu with fifteen legs of "bush deer." When the suitor asks for his wife, he takes twenty cocoanuts, twenty kola, fourteen yams, two legs of "bush deer," and a calabash of oil. These are shared among the family of the girl who promised to send her in three months.

D

No money is paid for a wife who is betrothed in child-hood, but in the case of a second marriage a money payment is required. A woman who has a child waits one year before she marries again, and her father receives twelve shillings in cowries. As mentioned above, a childless woman is not free to marry as she pleases; she remains in the family of her late husband, and passes either to one of his brothers or to one of the sons, if they are adult. The man to whom she is allotted takes a goat and calls the family together, the head of the family kills the goat to the idioñ and a small boy roasts it. Then all sit down. When the fufu and the goat's meat are brought a second sacrifice is offered the deceased ancestors, and the head of the family declares " we leave this girl to you."

It has been mentioned above that in parts of the area occupied by the Edo-speaking peoples the wife is not the property of the husband. In the Edo territory proper relationships between the sexes are found which correspond to some degree with this kind of marriage but confer no legal rights; the children remain under all circumstances in the family of the girl unless she actually goes to live with the man. One case came under my notice in which a woman was living with a man in her father's village and had borne three children; her father refused to recognise the marriage, but I was unable to ascertain whether he would claim the children if the husband predeceased him, and what the situation would be if the woman left the man.

This relationship, or more temporary unions, are well recognised among the Edo. A man alludes to the woman as ose, friend. It is by no means infrequent for married women to leave their husbands and live, sometimes for years, in relationships of this nature; unless, however, the bride price has been duly paid the woman and all her children belong to the husband *de jure*.

Originally it appears this relationship of friendship was an innocent one. I was told at Eviakoi that if a small girl wished to have a friend before she had a suitor, when a small boy looked at her and sent her a message, she would send a present back to him and they would go and salute each other.

At certain seasons of the year the girl would send food or money to the boy, and in return the boy would be required to send cloth or a handkerchief.

This went on until the girl had got a husband, and if their relationship had been perfectly innocent, it was customary for her former friend to become a suitor for, or receive as a wife, her eldest daughter. If, however, she should bear a child to her friend after a suitor has appeared for her hand, the child would go with her to her husband and a fine of £2 or more would be inflicted upon the offending " friend."

As to the position, however, of an illegitimate child, in cases of this sort there appears to be a certain amount of doubt. In other parts of the country I was informed that no suitor would marry a girl who had so misconducted herself, and that the bride price would have to be repaid.

It has been mentioned above that many women live openly with their lovers. Cases are of course equally frequent, if not more so, in which the husband is kept in ignorance. If a husband suspects his wife he reports the case to the head of his family, who takes her to a diviner. The diviner throws cowries, and if these fall in a certain way he pronounces her guilty, but she will deny the offence. She is then forced to kneel down in a chalk circle and the ita ordeal is tried. This is illegal under British rule, but it is no doubt frequently tried. One case actually came under my notice during my tour. The diviner says if she has ever committed adultery since she was given to her husband, let ita hold her ; if not, may ita let her go free. Then a fowl feather is passed through the middle of her tongue, three attempts are made to withdraw it, and if it is firmly fixed there she is pronounced guilty. She must then name her paramour, and may be flogged till she does so. Having done so she swears by Ake, Olokun, or her husband's father, that she is speaking the truth.

She buys a big goat for her husband to sacrifice to his father, the money for which she gets from her paramour, her father, or perhaps her husband, or she may have to sell her property, cloth, beads, etc., or what she makes by trade. Until this sacrifice has been made she may not eat from the same pot as her husband or her children ; if she did so the latter would fall sick.

If the husband meets the paramour he flogs him and tears his clothes off; but if the paramour meets the husband, he may hide in the bush, and the husband can pass on. If the husband is a big man he claims damages from the paramour ; he will send friends to his house and there they are offered kola or tobacco ; they then explain the object of their visit, and if he admits his share, he must be prepared to come to terms. If not, he buys two fowls, and takes them before Ogun or Oxwaie and swears. The wife may then be summoned to back up her charge, and if he now confesses he may have to pay £5 or more ; then he calls on the husband and eats kola with him ; before they do so they put Ogun between them and the man swears to keep away from the woman in future.

In some families a woman does not undergo the ordeal of ita ; she is compelled by her husband's ancestors to go and confess to him ; if she did not do so, she would fall sick or die suddenly.

When a woman confesses to adultery her husband passes an eggshell round her head from right to left and hangs it under the eaves of the house ; if she is solicited by a man she confesses to her husband, and the same ceremony is performed.

At Ijeba, just north of the Ora country, the bride price is about £3. If a wife objects to her husband she cannot repay the bride price and leave him, nor can her father do so unless she runs away to another man. The recognised procedure is for the wife to run to her father's house. From there she goes to the man she wants to marry, and the original husband comes to the house of his father-in-law to ask what has become of her. When he hears what has happened he goes to the king, who summons all the parties concerned. If the man to whom she has run can repay the bride price she is at liberty to go to him, otherwise she must go back. She has certain property in her husband's house: if she leaves it behind her she cannot claim it, but if she takes it with her to her father's house she may retain it.

At Okpe, when a woman bears a daughter a man takes five cowries, a pot of palm oil, and a pile of firewood to her father, and if the father agrees, he is recognised as a suitor. In addition to work a bride price of ten shillings is payable. If the girl refuses her suitor the bride price is repaid, but, as usual, there is no allowance for the work. If, however, she runs away after being married there is no refund if she goes to her father's house, and only half the price is refunded if she runs to another man. In some respects, therefore, the marriage at Okpe resembles the second of the types mentioned at the outset.

There is another point in which it also comes very close to the Isomi marriage: if a woman marries out of Okpe her body must be brought back to be buried.

The women of Okpe seem to be far more moral, according to European lights, than those of the tribes of the south. It seems to be exceedingly rare for a girl to bear a child before marriage.

It is a somewhat singular thing that the operation of clitoridectomy is known and practised in all the tribes to the south of Okpe. In Okpe it is known but not practised, and precisely here is the standard of morality higher.

At Sabongida the customs as to the bride price do not differ essentially from those already noted, save that in certain cases it appears to be paid in part after marriage.

If a woman leaves her husband and practises free love, she is not required, as among the Edo, to name the offenders. When she goes back to her husband she says to him, " I can't cook for you," and the husband asks why. She replies, " Some people hold my cloth." Thereupon the husband answers, " Go and get a cock." This she does, and her husband sacrifices it.

Here, free love before marriage is so far legalised that, according to one informant, a payment is made to the mother of a girl before she enters into relations with a man.

In the kingdom of Agbede much the same conditions appear to prevail until we get near the eastern boundaries. At Idegun, however, the marriage customs are clearly influenced by those of the Ida districts. There are two kinds of wives, one called Ame, who is the wife proper, but is never obtained in Idegun itself; the other called Ose, who corresponds to the " friend" of the Edo country. In Idegun apparently the children of an Ose wife belong to her father; elsewhere in the Ishan districts different rules prevail, and the children are sometimes divided. There is no penalty for an Ose wife who commits adultery, and the offending man is fined ninepence or a shilling. If, on the other hand, an Ame wife was proved guilty the offending man was formerly sold as a slave, and the woman paid a goat and a small fowl to her husband and was flogged by the women of the compound.

When we come to the Kukuruku of Ida we find the two types of marriage alluded to at the outset existing side by side. The Amoiya wife is absolutely bound to the husband, and, in fact, in some places only slaves became Amoiya wives. Her children are his heirs, and under no circumstances does she pass out of the family, though she may, if the husband be impotent, be temporarily assigned to another man, who must not be a member of the family. She remains with him until the death of the husband, when she passes to the heirs in the ordinary course of things.

The Isomi, on the other hand, as already mentioned, is free to leave her husband practically at any time. Her children take property from her family and not from their father, unless (a) the father pays £30 requisite to make his son by an Isomi wife a chief, or (b) unless a son after his father's death elects to remain in his father's country and to take a share of his father's property.

In connection with marriage at Okpe, it has been mentioned that custom requires the husband of an Okpe woman who has married out of her own country to send her body back for burial under penalty of a fine. Precisely the same practice prevails with regard to the Isomi wife, whose body must be returned to her own family. In some places the bodies of children too must be handed over. Elsewhere, the rights of the father appear to be supplanting the rights of the mother's family, and property in the children remains with the father.

In dealing with the marriages from this part of the country, another point must be mentioned, namely, the exogamous classes of the Wefa country, known by the name of Egǫ and Atzikia. According to traidtion, these classes were formed when the present inhabitants immigrated from the Sobo country some hundreds of years ago. The rule is that no man may marry a woman of his own class; the children of an Amoiya wife belong to the exogamous class of the husband, and the same is the case if the wife has come from another tribe. The children of an Isemi wife belong to the woman's class. If the child of an Isomi wife elects to remain in his father's country, he does not by so doing change his matrimonial class.

At Fuga, in the case of the Isomi marriage, a man begs for a girl, and if he is accepted he helps his father-in-law in the farm work ; the father-in-law gives food to the workers, the suitor sends palm nuts for the mother, fetches water, fire, etc. The bride price is £5 or less, and when it is paid the husband and friends fetch the girl home; the goat is given to the girl; it is not killed, but sent to her father's house The husband's compound goes at daybreak to salute his father-in-law and mother-in-law, and her mother cooks fufu and sends it to her husband's house. The wife gets no presents from her father or mother. At daybreak she takes a broom and sweeps the house; ten days later she begins going to farm ; she lives with her husband's mother or elder wife, but if she misbehaves herself she gets a house of her own, otherwise she can stay until her children are old enough to work. Half the bride price of the Isomi wife goes to the mother's father, half to the girl's father. A son belongs either to the wife's father or to his own father (if the father makes him a chief).

In the case of Amoiya marriage, a girl is usually made an Amoiya wife by the orders of a diviner, and the payment is twenty-five measures or five pounds. Anyone can buy an Amoiya wife; she is usually four or five years old, and the purchaser takes her with him. All children belong to the husband, and there is no further ceremony. If a girl for whom a man is paying bride price bears a child before marriage, the bride price must be repaid by the man to whom she bears the child, and the original suitor cannot marry her.

If an Amoiya wife commits adultery the offender pays five slaves, or their value, to the husband and one to each big chief. The husband buys a goat to sacrifice to his ancestors, which is eaten by the family, but not by himself or his wife.

In the case of the Isomi wife a goat is paid to the husband, who may, if he chooses, assault the offender. Otherwise the woman's lover buys a goat, a cock, a tortoise, a dog, a snail, and a small chicken which the husband sacrifices, but not to his father.

These two kinds of marriage appear to prevail throughout the country as far as Auči. Something must be said with regard to the bride price payable for the children. The descendants of the Amoiya wife are the absolute property of the husband. Consequently he receives the whole of the bride price paid for the daughters, and the mother's family gets no share.

If, however, a daughter of an Isomi wife is to be given to a suitor, about five-eighths of the price will go to the mother's family and three-eighths to the father's family, but only a small proportion of this would actually remain in the hands of the father or mother.

It should also be mentioned that if the children of an

Isomi wife die one after the other, the husband asks her family to sell her to him as an Amoiya wife, and they have no option but to agree.

When we cross the border into Northern Nigeria these two kinds of marriage are still found for a certain distance. In the Ibie country the name given to Isomi marriage is Agbele, while Amoiya is called Isogo.

The price of an Isomi wife is about five pounds, and all the people in the town are witnesses to the price. In addition to these, Enabǫ marriage is also known in which the wife comes from another country. If her husband dies, the Enabǫ widow must either marry his brother or return home. She is not permitted to marry another man of the same town. At Kominio, in the Upila country, the Isemi wife is called Ateme, the Amoiya wife is called Onawateva, and the customs are the same as in the Ibie country.

At Soso an entirely different state of things prevails. The people of Soso, according to what seems to be a well-founded tradition, appear to be immigrants who fled before the Nupe raiders. At the outset, according to their story, the place was colonised by five persons. There must have been at this time, and later, a great scarcity of women. This is probably the explanation of the Soso custom of child marriage. I saw several wives who were reported to have been married at least three years, and they none of them appeared to be more than thirteen years old at the outside. I could not, however, observe the slightest ill-effects of this premature marriage, on the contrary, both young and older wives, appeared to be particularly healthy, and the standard of physical development was a good one.

If a wife dislikes her husband, the case is taken before the chief, and if good reasons are given, the bride price is repaid and old men act as arbitrators to decide the amount. If, however, the wife has borne a child to her husband nothing is repayable—the marriage therefore, in this respect, is on a par with the Isomi union ; it appears, however, that even when a child has been born, the formalities have to be carried out. The court fee for a separation order is payable half by the wife, half by the husband. Widows are free to go home, and the second husband pays the same bride price as the first. Wives are brought from outside as in other places, but I was informed that no Soso girl ever marries out of her own country. At Semolika the marriage customs appear to resemble those of Okpe. Girls are married all at the same season of the year, and in the place of being taken home by conductors from their own family they are brought to the husbands, as at Kominio, by the company of the husband. If a wife runs away no bride price is repayable if she has borne children. The customs with regard to adultery are the same as at Okpe. There appears to be no recognised penalty, but the injured husband is compelled by custom to commit adultery with the wife of the man who has committed adultery with his own wife. Should the offender not be married, the husband may settle the matter by selecting the wife either of the man's brother or of his father. Or he may elect to wait until the man's marriage. Should he die in the meantime, the quarrel descends to his brother, and the matter is not considered settled until retribution has been done. At Ibilo again the Isomi custom prevails, and the wife is taken home by the friends of the husband. At Isua two slightly different forms of marriage prevail, one in the upper quarter, one in the lower quarter, but the differences are only in detail.

In the Sobo country entirely different conditions prevail. In the greater part of the country with which we have been hitherto concerned, monogamy is rare except in the case of poor men, and two husbands out of five on an average will be found to have two wives. In the Sobo country, on the other hand, it seems to be exceedingly rare to find a husband with more than one wife. In the Sobo country the wife is the absolute property of the husband, and there is no question of her leaving her husband and repaying the bride price.

Again, in the remainder of the territory of the Edo-speaking people, it appears to be rare to put pressure upon a girl to marry a suitor to whom she objects, but in the Sobo country, owing possibly to the considerably higher money payments as part of the bride price, and to the consequent greater difficulty of refunding the bride price, it appears to be the custom to compel a girl to accept a suitor. I was told at Okwoloho that if a girl was unwilling it would make a quarrel between the two families. The suitor would seize some of her father's family and the father would put pressure on her to consent. When she did so the pawns would be returned, and husband received one case of gin as a payment for the people who helped to seize the pawns. In a marriage under these circumstances there are no conductors.

If a girl runs from her husband the bride price may be repaid, but the husband applies in the first instance to the girl's mother. The father tries to induce her to go back, but if he does not succeed he is responsible for the bride price. If a child has been born and the bride price is repaid the child appears to go with the mother contrary to the usual custom.

In the Sobo country there is a curious custom which suggests that we have to do with a transitional form. There are a certain number of peoples whose custom requires that a husband should go and reside with his wife's family. This is called matrilocal marriage. There are other peoples again among whom the wife at once goes to reside with the husband. Between the two we have other peoples in which the husband resides for a time with his wife's people and then removes to his own district.

The Sobo custom is a variation of this, for the husband does not, strictly speaking, live with his wife's people, but only visits his wife every evening at her father's house, and leaves again at daybreak; this goes on for about three months, and then the girl is conducted to her husband's house by members of her own family, precisely as is done among others of the Edo-speaking people before the marriage is consummated.

There is, however a further variation in parts of the Sobo

territory. At Ajeyubi the new wife remains in her husband's house for three months, and the head wife has to cook for her if her husband already has a wife. Then she dresses to go and see her mother, taking with her a present of the value of ten shillings, and a calabash of oil to be shared between her mother and father. Nine days later she returns to her husband and receives a present from him of the value of one pound. Then she stays one month with her husband, and her husband's father comes to make her a present which may be anything between one shilling and five pounds. At the end of the month she goes to see her father again, and stays nine days; she takes nothing with her. Then she stays four days with her husband; he gives her four shillings and a pot of oil to give her father. On the fifth day she goes back to her father and remains with him for nine days. On her return she goes into the bush to collect firewood, puts it down outside her husband's house and lights a fire inside. Four days later she goes back to her father again, and stays a month or rather less. He receives from her two shillings and a bottle of gin, and she takes back a bundle of firewood.

This concludes the formalities, and the wife now receives a house from her husband, who also takes her to the bush. shows her her farms, and cleans them for her.

At Iyede there is yet another variation; when a wife conceives for the first time she goes back to her mother for three days. On her return she occupies a house which her husband builds for her, but four or five months later she returns to her mother, and remains there until the child is three months old. Then the husband takes a calabash of oil and sees his child for the first time. The oil with some fish is given to the wife's father and mother, and the husband is at liberty to take her home.

The explanation of these customs appears to be that the wife is not regarded as having passed entirely into the possession of the husband until a child is born. This seems to follow clearly from the customs of Iyede. If this is the case, then the journeying backwards and forwards of the wife and the payments by the husband are a transitional stage between the custom which makes her his property only when she has borne a child and that which finally gives her over to him when the purchase money is paid.

Marriage Prohibitions.—Over the whole area occupied by the Edo-speaking people, the ordinary rule of prohibited degrees is that a man may not marry a woman who belongs either to his father's or his mother's family. Precisely how far the limits of the family extend is difficult to ascertain. It seems to be clear that no marriage will be permitted where any family relationship is recognised, but it seems to be equally clear that, after a certain point, a family breaks up. In certain communities the test of membership of a family is whether they sacrifice to the ancestors in the same place. In the kingdom of Edo, so far as the father's family is concerned, the test is a simpler one. The majority of families have a totem, known as Awa or Awaigbe, that is, family prohibition or totem. The totem may be an animal, a plant, an object of domestic use, or a certain action or form of words. The plant or animal may not be eaten nor used, and the form of words or object is likewise forbidden to be used. Only during the burial ceremonies are these prohibitions relaxed. These prohibitions descend from father to child, and in no case is a man married to a woman who has the same prohibitions as himself.

There are other prohibitions, known as Awailimi, which are imposed by the priest. Occasionally it may be found that two people with the same prohibitions marry, but in this case the explanation always is that the prohibitions in question have been imposed on one or both sides by the priest.

It is important to note that, although a man must marry a woman who has the same prohibitions as himself, his wives, so long as they are married to him or are suckling his children, are forbidden to eat this prohibited food, or in any way infringe his Awaigbe. It is an interesting question how far this rule extends to the case of a mother of illegitimate children ; enquiry should also be made whether such children take their Awaigbe from their father or from their mother. On the analogy of the case of the Isomi children in the Ida districts, we should expect the descent to be through the mother.

Although it is in many places a rule that a man may not marry anyone in his father's family, there are exceptions both in the Edo district and elsewhere. The most frequent of these is that a man is permitted to marry his half sister by the same father. This is the rule at Gwaton in the Edo country, and at Ososo. In the latter case it may be put down as an exception either to a scarcity of women, which as we have seen must have prevailed formerly, or to the influence of the tribes to the north among whom such marriages appear to be permitted.

With regard to the observance as distinct from the existence of these marriage rules, it is somewhat difficult to collect information. At Gwaton and elsewhere I found rules as to the purification to be undergone by people who had married in spite of the rules. Quite apart from that, it appears to be a well-established fact that sexual relations between people forbidden to marry are in many cases by no means uncommon. At Sabongida, when I put the question to the old men, I was told that such unions were quite unknown. When, however, I consulted an independent witness who was not a native of the place, but was well acquainted with the people, he was able to cite five or six cases of such unions, and the parties, on being questioned, admitted the circumstances quite frankly.

BIRTH.—The birth customs vary widely from tribe to tribe, but they are of comparatively small importance, except from a strictly scientific point of view. Only occasionally are mother and child subject to tabus of any sort. As a rule, though the child may not be taken out of the house at once, and may not be taken to the farm for some three months after birth, the regulations as to intercourse with members of the household or strangers are far from severe.

Parturition appears to be an easy matter in most cases, though a certain number of difficult cases occur which in the old days, and often at the present day result in death of mother and child.

There are seldom regulations as to the place in which birth is to occur, and in the Edo country it is by no means uncommon to see by the roadside a small tree which marks the spot where a child has been born.

Mother and child are usually washed outside the house by an attendant woman or women, and the child is brought back with various ceremonies, such as the beating of calabashes, and handed to the mother. As a rule, though infant mortality is heavy, mothers appear to care for their children well. Of the non-lethal accidents to which the child is subject, the most important is umbilical hernia, which is extremely prevalent in some parts of the country, but in other parts almost unknown.

A child is weaned after about seven or eight months, though suckling may go on for a considerable time longer. It is by no means uncommon to see children of four or five years of age sharing their mother's breasts with a younger child. Apparently the duration of suckling has little affect upon the fecundity of the women. There appear to be no special regulations regulating the period of continence to be observed after birth, it varies from three months to two years.

SECTION IV.

INHERITANCE, ADOPTION, AND PROPERTY.

INHERITANCE.—Broadly speaking, the scheme of inheritance is the same for the whole of the Edo-speaking people, if we except such cases as those of the children of an Isomi wife, to which allusion has already been made in connection with marriage customs. A man's legal heirs are his own children.

We may distinguish three groups of customs of inheritance. In the first group the heir is the eldest son, whom we may conveniently distinguish as the "head son." If his brothers and sisters, either of whole or of half blood, receive any of the dead man's estate, it is only by an act of grace on the part of the legal heir. In the second place, as in Edo itself, there are a group of heirs, though the head son still takes the major share; as joint-heirs he has with him the eldest sons by the other wives of his father. These may be distinguished as the "senior sons." Finally, we have a comparatively small group in which all the children, male or female, divide the property.

Combined with these customs in various degrees, which change in many cases according to the age of the children entitled to the property, is the right of the father's brothers, or brother, to a share in the inheritance. Sometimes he can lay claim to the whole of the property, and takes possession of the children; in other cases he is simply the guardian and has at most a restricted right of usage of the property, though he cannot in every case be called to account where he has lost the property by trading or otherwise.

Where no sons are left the property sometimes passes to

the father's brother, sometimes to a daughter, or different kinds of property may be inherited, some by the brother, some by the daughter.

The statement that among the Edo-speaking peoples a man's children are his heirs, is subject to two further qualifications. In the first place, where a murder had been committed it was the rule for the murderer or homicide to pay one or more persons to the family of the murdered man. The substitutes took the place of the dead man in every respect. If the murdered man was the eldest son of the family, the adopted child would be the chief heir. The adopted child sacrifices to his new father and mother, not to his old one. Only in one respect does his relationship to his old family come out, and that is with regard to marriage customs. A man thus transferred by " penal adoption," as it may be termed, from one family to another, is prohibited from marrying into either the old or the new family. In some cases, however, the prohibition with regard to the family from which he came lapses after one generation.

The second exception to the rule of inheritance is formed by the case of the illegitimate child of a woman, subsequently married to a man who is not the father of the child. In some of the tribes such a child would not go to the husband ; in others he might go to the husband, but would not be reckoned as the heir ; in other cases he appears to enter the family of his mother's husband, and enjoy all the rights that he would enjoy if he were actually the child of that husband.

In this connection it may be well to mention, though cases are rare in which the matter is of importance, that where no legitimate heirs are found there is or was a custom in the kingdom of Edo of making a man's illegitimate children his heirs. This is not really an exception to the customs of the Edo-speaking peoples, for a woman who bears such a child is practically in the position of an Isomi wife, and, as has been pointed out under " marriage customs," the child of an Isomi wife may take his inheritance from his mother's people, or may elect to remain in his father's country and become his heir.

One other point remains to be mentioned in this general survey. In the north-eastern portion of the Edo-speaking country customs of inheritance are complicated—firstly, by questions of age, and secondly, by ceremonial observances. A man's sons are not his heirs, unless they are older than any of his brothers' sons. This custom is known in pidgin English as " big-and-big." But even if a son is entitled to succeed under this rule, he cannot take his father's property unless he has joined the Otu, or company of young men.

The rules with regard to a woman's property are virtually the same, save that brothers have no rights except in the absence of children.

Under ordinary circumstances a man's property in the kingdom of Edo goes to the eldest sons by each wife; and in some cases the head son gets the biggest share.

At Eviakoi small things are given to the rest of the children, and after them the eldest sons divide the rest.

At Ugo there seem to be three different rules. In some families the property is divided in the ordinary way; in others all the sons take a share ; and in others the head son, *i.e.*, the eldest son of all, takes the property and his brothers come and live with him and get any share which he chooses to give them.

At Usen the head son gets the property, but the others also get shares. If a brother lived in the house of the dead man and worked for him without payment in his lifetime, he would also get a share of the deceased's property. Failing sons, the property will go to a brother by the same father and the same mother, and the eldest will probably get a big share. Brothers by the same father rank next.

Failing brothers of any sort, the head of the family succeeds. In some cases, for example, at Gwatoñ, a daughter takes a share if there is no son by her mother. In this case the brother of the father might come and stay in the house with the daughter.

In Edo itself the king, and in some villages the ogie, was heir, and in some cases, at any rate, he appeared to rank before the head of the family and after brothers. In Edo I was informed that both brothers and sisters inherit from a childless man. I got no confirmation of this statement, and it was contradicted, the reason being given that a woman belongs to another family after marriage. The father never takes the property.

The story is told of a chief who died in the time of Esẹmede without legitimate children. Esẹmede said he could not take the property for the house would then be extinct; but it was found that the man had a child by a friend and this boy succeeded. It ·appears to be an ordinary rule at the present time that if a woman has an illegitimate child it stays with her till it is grown up, and then it goes to its father, but, at any rate at Okolo, an illegitimate child before a marriage is not the heir.

An old man who has much property will sometimes make a will or rather divide his property before his death. If he is not head of the family, he calls the head of the family and all his sons and daughters and divides his goods. Then Echwai and Osun are brought out and put in Aluerha (the shrine of the father) and anyone who violates the arrangement is cursed. I was told that if no member of the man's father's family survived the property may go to his mother's family but this again was not confirmed. It must be understood that it is exceedingly rare to find cases in which a man has not a good many relatives. As mentioned under adoption a certain number of cases were found and where there were no heirs there seemed to be much uncertainty as to who would succeed to the property. Unfortunately in all the cases of heirless men that I met with in the kingdom of Edo the men themselves were absent and I was unable to ascertain from them what the probable course of events would be. It may be added that when the question is put in an abstract form, "What happens when a man dies without children or brothers or sisters?" the invariable reply is "Such things never happen in our country," though in point of fact they seem to be not uncommon in certain parts. It will of course be understood that the property of a man who has no visible heirs is rarely large.

With regard to widows the ordinary rule is that those women who have borne children and whose children survive are free. The childless widows or those whose children are dead form part of the property to be divided at death. Where the children are small the widow or widows will often go to a brother of the deceased, and he, when the children grew up, would often provide a wife for the eldest son. The guardian of small children is commonly the brother of the deceased man.

In Ugo in the king's family the king is the guardian, otherwise the " big man " in the neighbourhood of the house.

If some of the sons are small and the head son is adult he is guardian for his brothers. In point of fact it by no means follows that the guardian carries out his duties, and cases have been quoted to me in which children who were small at the time of their father's death have lost all their property. In theory the guardian is free to sell animals, or to consume perishable property, such as yams, but all the rest should be kept till the children are grown up.

At Gwaton a posthumous child belongs to the head of the family. The mother does not marry again till the child is born and mother or sisters may act as guardians.

At Eviakoi the posthumous child may be the heir if there are no other children.

At Usen the posthumous child would share with its other brothers, and the same is the case at Okolo.

With regard to a woman's property, if she has no children, it will go to her brother, who will give some to the rest of the family and worship her as a mother in addition to his own mother. He must call the name of the adopted mother first or he will fall sick.

At Gwaton I was told that if a widow has no children, any trees which she owns will go to her brother by the same father and mother.   He will also take all that she brought from her father's house.   I was told that the husband is the owner of anything which is made by a wife in his house, but what would happen to such property after the death of the husband I did not discover.   It will probably pass with the rest of the property, so far as it was made before the death of the husband, and after that time, it would be the property of the woman herself and would pass to her brother.

At Eviakoi the brother who buries a woman takes her property.

At Usen the property made by a woman in her husband's house goes to her brothers by the same father and mother, not to her husband.   If a woman has children both sons and daughters share the property or if there are only daughters they will take the whole.   Where there were any slaves they passed to the daughters.   They actually lived with the mother's brother, but all wealth produced by them belonged to the daughter.

At Usen all the children of a woman share but a big share goes to the eldest.

At Ijeba and in the Ora country and eastwards as far as Auči the customs are much the same.

At Ijeba the sons get the property but a larger share goes to the head son.   If there is a house the brothers can stay in it and bring their wives; but they are liable to be turned out by the head son if there is a quarrel.   The widows go to the sons but of course no son takes his own mother; the women appear to have some freedom of choice.   If there are no sons, own brothers succeed, failing them father's brothers.

The mother's brother never succeeds nor the father, but failing heirs the latter has usufruct.   A daughter may take the property, failing heirs, and she hands it to the head of the house; but apparently he has little or no control.

At Aroko the eldest sons of each of the wives share the property equally.   If there are no sons the next younger brother of the deceased man is his heir, or, failing the younger brother, the son of the elder brother.   A younger brother by the same father can take the property, failing the younger brother by the same father and mother. What a woman makes belongs to her husband. A man or woman without children may adopt brother's or sister's children.

At Okpe the eldest son, not necessarily by the head wife, gets all the property; but it is said that he ought to buy wives for his brothers. Failing a son a daughter can take the property. A brother succeeds a childless man. The widow is free if she has borne children.

At Otua the eldest sons of each wife are the heirs, but a daughter can get such things as cloth. The brothers of the head son cannot be turned out of the house, and add to it as necessary; they often cultivate the same farm and divide the produce. If a man has no sons his brother is the heir; daughters or sisters may inherit if there are no males. The property of an heirless man is inherited by the king.

At Sabongida the eldest sons take the property and the head son gets the house; the others can stay in the house or live near, and cannot be ejected. The yams on the farm are divided, and if a son is away his mother takes his share, or the head son keeps it for him, or it may be sold and the money handed over later. Failing sons a man's heir is his brother; failing brothers the head of the house.

A man may not give property to his wife, and both here and at Ijeba she swears on the dead body to hand over all the property she holds from her deceased husband.

At Afuje the eldest sons share the property. If one wife has daughters and no sons the daughter takes the place of a son. Failing children, brothers, then brothers' sons and then sisters are the next heirs. None of the wives are free.

At Ijeba a man or woman who has no children adopts the child of a brother. Failing a brother's or sister's child they may adopt any other person's child, but where the adopted child is not a member of the family it is not the heir.

At Ijeba a woman may make the king her heir. Then the king buries her; but a brother, if there is one, has a prior claim.

At Aroko a woman's property goes to her sons; failing sons to daughters, failing daughters to her brothers.

At Otua the husband owns what a woman produces. If she is unmarried it belongs to her father.

At Sabongida a woman's property goes to her son, failing sons to her daughters, failing daughters to brothers or sisters.

Agbede town and a few of the villages are now Mohammedan, the conversion dating back some fifteen years, though individuals professed this creed a good many years earlier. So far as I can discover the only customs to be affected by the change are those connected with the disposal of the dead, and, of course, the religious ceremonies. The division of property takes place three months after death. The first-born son takes a preferential share; after him the eldest sons of the wives and the head of the deceased's brothers (whether by the same mother or not is immaterial) take equal shares; if there is much property the other sons and brothers take in order. If property still remains after this a second round is begun. If the eldest son of any woman is small he gets his proper share, which is entrusted to the care of his mother. She in her turn hands it to her husband's brother, who is the legal heir of the dead man's widows, and takes her to wife. If any woman has daughters and no sons the eldest daughter takes the share, provided it is property that a woman can hold. Other daughters can take shares after sons and brothers have taken.

Where there are no children the deceased's firstborn brother (any wife) takes the property, but if there is much the other brothers take shares. But a daughter has a right to one share of yams before other heirs, to cloth and all women's things, e.g., some of the beads, some of the cloth, and some of the goats. Failing brothers the next heir is the odioekelafe or head of the "great family."

The wives go to the adult sons, the first choice lying with the firstborn; but he gets no extra share unless there are enough to go round. Failing adult sons deceased's brothers, *i.c.*, brother by the same father and mother, or by the same father and a different mother, take the wives. Where there are no brothers the wives have freedom of choice ; they do not pass with the rest of the property.

At Idua the rule appears to be that the sons inherit in any case, the largest share falling to the firstborn ; if they are young they wait till they are grown up before they take their shares, which are till then in the hands of the head of the family. It is the guardian's duty to pay and collect debts ; he may use the money but must repay it to the heirs and use his own money to pay the bride-price for them. If he loses the money there is no means of restraining him.

Failing sons, the daughters can inherit, subject to the usual condition as to the kind of property. In this case the mother or eldest brother is said to be the guardian ; but in some cases at least the head of the house is her guardian, and when a daughter marries she must apply to him before he hands the property over to her.

The younger sons seem to have no well defined rights, but it is stated that the eldest buys wives for them and that he will also make presents to his sisters.

The younger brothers have a right to reside in the father's house, but build their own houses when they marry. Garden farms, or small plantations of tobacco or plantains near the house, are known but not common ; they fall to the firstborn ; the produce of other farms is got in before it is divided. The wives go to the sons but those who have borne children are free.

At Jagbe the property is divided seven days after death ; the firstborn takes the largest share and his brothers' shares are proportioned to their ages to some extent ; only the eldest sons of the wives take shares.

Failing sons the daughters take some of the property and the brother of the deceased by the same mother (Bfm)[1] takes the remainder, the head of the town being responsible for dividing it. This brother also succeeds to the remainder

[1] See p. 151.

of the property if there are no daughters. If there are no brothers (Bfm or Bf) the head of the family is the heir.

The wives go to the sons, but if they are small, the women may be given to anyone either inside or outside the family, and these second husbands, when the sons reach manhood, either make them presents or purchase wives for them.

At Idegun the firstborn gets the biggest share and the eldest sons of the wives are joint heirs. The house and garden farm go to the firstborn, but his brothers can share in the produce of the latter if they apply to the firstborn. The joint heirs take yams from the farm as they need them; they can also sell them and either share the money or use it to pay the debts of the deceased.

If any wife has no son, her daughter takes in his place, but such things as guns or cutlasses go to the brother by the same mother (Bfm), failing him to a brother of the deceased by the same father (Bf). A daughter can own a cocoanut tree but her father's brother is the custodian of it, he may at will be replaced by another man. If dowry has been paid for a girl, she takes no share.

The widow's position depends on whether they are natives of Idegun or not, i.e., upon whether she is a non-dowry or a dowry wife. There is a prejudice in Idegun against receiving the bride-price except from strangers, the result is that the women who marry in Idegun are in the position of ose or mistresses (the same term is used by other Edo-speaking peoples of the woman who enters into pre- or extra-matrimonial connections). Where no bride price has been paid, the sons or brothers have no claim on the widow, conversely the married woman for whom dowry has been paid can not lay claim to property devolving from her own family. The widow can marry three months after her husband's death, and her children reckon as brothers and sisters of the second marriage; but they have no claim to any share of the property of the second husband.

Where there are no sons or eligible daughters, the brother of the deceased by the same or another mother (Bfm or Bf) is the heir, and he also takes the house where daughters only survive.

At Ewori the rules are the same, save that the widows pass in the ordinary way, the first-born may get three or four, when his brothers have one each; the deceased's brother (Bfm or Bf) may also take some.

At Ama, on the other hand, the first-born is sole heir, though it is the custom for him to make presents to his brothers and sisters, and the widows are divided. Failing sons the brother by the same mother (Bfm) is the heir, but he likewise may make presents to the daughters. If there are no brothers by the same or other mothers (Bfm or Bf), the head of the family succeeds and the town buries the dead man. This brings with it no liability with regard to debts.

At Uzia the eldest sons of the wives are the heirs, and they are limited to their next brothers when they make presents of portions of their shares; if there are only small sons or none, the brother (Bfm or Bf) of the deceased succeeds as elsewhere, but he can make presents of cloth and other woman's things to adult daughters; small children pass to him with the widows.

At Awoiki the property is divided three or four months after death; the first-born is the heir, but he can make presents to his adult brothers. If the sons are small, the eldest brother of the deceased (Bfm or Bf) succeeds; he is at liberty to spend the inheritance, but if any remains when the first-born reaches manhood the brother must hand it over to him. Adult daughters have, in the absence of sons, a right to some of the property.

In the Eda country, near Akeke, property is divided on the fifth day after death, the first-born takes a large share and is guardian of the property of the senior sons till they reach manhood. If there are no grown sons, the brother (Bfm or Bf) takes the property, but gives presents at a later stage. The eldest daughter can claim cloth, goats, etc., as a right in the absence of sons. Failing children or brothers the head of the family is the heir.

At Ekwe the sons and brothers meet on the fifth day after death, and the property is shared out to males and females in order of age; the first-born can claim the house and farms, but the head of the family has first choice of movable goods.

The wives and small children go to the adult sons, but any child whose teeth have appeared can claim his share of the property. The debts of the deceased are paid by a levy of equal contributions from brothers and sons; the property is divided before the debts are paid.

At Woriki the first-born takes his share, then the eldest sons, and, if there is sufficient, all the other sons, but the brothers (Bfm and Bf) take precedence of them, at least as regards cloth, goats, and probably other movables. In the absence of sons a daughter can take woman's things; if there are no sons by any wife, the brother (Bfm or Bf) is the heir, but daughters take woman's things, which are stated to be cloth, goats, cowries, etc., though the first two of these were enumerated among the brothers' shares where there were sons. Failing sons and brothers the king of the town is the heir.

The first-born gets the house and garden farm; the farm property is divided when the yams are tied; two ropes go to the head of the family, then the sons get their shares, then the brothers.

The guardian is, according to circumstances, the eldest brother by the same mother, or the mother, if there is no adult brother.

The wives may all fall to the first-born if there are few, or he may get two or three, his brothers one each, and his father's brothers the remainder.

At Yaju the first line of heirs consists of the first-born, the senior sons and the brother; daughters succeed to yams, cloth, beads, etc., where there are no male heirs. The wives are divided first, then movables, then trees and farms; the yams are tied up first, two ropes fall to the brother, the rest to the sons, and they may agree to keep them as a common stock and farm in common.

The widows go to the first-born, if few, but something depends on whether he has wives already ; the women themselves have also some voice in the matter.

It may be mentioned here that in small rivers each family owns a stretch of water and the eldest son inherits the rights.

Where "penal adoption" (the payment of a substitute for a murdered man) takes place, the rules of inheritance seem in nearly every case to be unaffected by the change ; the substitute steps into the dead man's shoes except at Idegun, where he cannot be head son.

In all cases where I put the question, viz., at Eda, Ekwe, and Woriki, the illegitimate child brought by a wife to her husband reckons as his first son. The rules with regard to posthumous children are more varied, the mere fact of their being posthumous does not appear to affect their status, unless they are born after the property is divided; this is the case in Agbede town and Yaju. At Jagbe, where the property is divided at the conclusion of the burial ceremonies, the posthumous son gets nothing from his father's estate, his stepfather (*i.e.,* B f) calls him brother, but a share of the estate falls to the stepson, though not so large a share as the eldest son *de facto* receives. If, however, the wife does not marry a son or brother of the deceased, the posthumous son gets the big share. The bride-price for a posthumous daughter goes to the stepfather.

At Idegun the posthumous son gets something from the estate, and his mother is the guardian. At Ewori the child gets something from his brothers when he reaches manhood, and something from his stepbrother. At Ama, Eda, Ekwe, and Woriki the posthumous child gets no share.

Turning now to women's property, it may be noted that there is some variation in the rules as to what property a woman may hold, at Agbede, Idegun, and Woriki[1] they may own cocoanut trees, while at Jagbe these are forbidden them, though they may own plantain.

---

[1] See also *infra.*

In Agbede the property of a married woman goes to her children, the daughters taking the women's things; the first-born son gets a big share; the husband takes all if there are no children. At Idua the same rule as to children seems to apply, but a married daughter gets no share. Failing children the property reverts to a woman's family.

In Idegun a woman's property goes to her children, the largest share falling to the first-born son. If there are no children the husband takes all that the woman has made in his house; the remainder goes back to her family, the heirs being (1) brother, (2) sister, or (3) father's brother; the father and mother never inherit.

At Ama the heir is the eldest son; the eldest daughter may succeed if there is no son; after them the husband takes all. The same rule applies at Uzia, but the daughter only takes pots and the like, the rest going to the husband, whatever its source. If the husband is dead a widow can hand the property during her lifetime to her daughters; if she has no children she can return to her father's house with her property, which remains in her family when she dies.

At Awoiki the property of a non-dowry wife returns to her family whether she has children or not. The dowry-wife's estate passes to her eldest son, failing him to her husband; if her husband is dead her brother succeeds, but the daughter can claim the cooking pots.

At Ewori the children share the property; failing children it goes to the husband.

At Eda the heirs are (1) the son, (2) the daughter, who can hand some to her father, and (3) the brother, who in any case takes what the woman has made with her own hands.

At Ekwe the sons and daughters are heirs, failing them the husband.

At Woriki the first-born gets his share, then other sons; cooking pots fall to the daughters. If there are no sons the husband takes what has been made in his house, and the brother the remainder. A woman should leave to her sons such things as slaves, cows, guns, cocoanut trees, from which it may be inferred that here women had extensive rights ; elsewhere these kinds of property are, as a rule, forbidden to women.

At Yaju the head son takes the property, the next heirs are the daughters (woman's things) and the husband. If there are no children the husband takes all, save what the woman brought from her father's house.

The duties associated with inheritance are few. The deceased is buried by his heirs, and conversely. The man who buries a debtor or heirless man takes over debts or property, as the case may be.

The duty of sacrificing to the dead man falls upon his children, whether they or his brothers are his heirs. In fact, the sacrifice seems to be looked upon rather as a means of keeping sickness or other misfortune away from the children than as a duty imposed by pious regard.

In certain cases the first-born has duties towards his brothers, such as that of permitting them to reside in his house ; but here again it is less a duty than a privilege, for they increase his importance and add to his wealth. As a matter of course the sister remains with her brother till marriage, and this too adds to his wealth, for he receives the bride-price, commonly known in West Africa by the un-fortunate name of dowry.

At Irua, in the Ishan country, the ordinary rule is that the head son takes a big share and then other brothers, according to age ; daughters get such property as goats. The eldest or head son may be a guardian for small children, or their mother may look after their property. In the absence of sons the house goes to the deceased's brother, and the movable property only goes to the daughters. If there are no other heirs the king takes the property. Debts are paid by the head son aided by the others.

Widows go to the head son, but he can give them to adult brothers.

At Igiawe the head son takes all the property but he can give presents to his brothers ; the next heirs are the brothers of the deceased unless there are unmarried daughters; an unmarried daughter becomes arhewa and remains in the house, to which her father's brother may come, if he has none of his own; if she has not been given to a husband before the father's death, a girl cannot marry; she is, however, at liberty to have as many lovers as she pleases, and her eldest son takes her property. Widows go to the head son; if there are no sons, to the father's brother.

The brother of a deceased man acts as guardian of the property; if there are young wives, they may be reserved for the son and in the meantime have lovers, whose children belong to the son.

At Ewu the head son takes the property; he can give a share to his father's brother and his sisters, the deceased's brothers, then the head of the family rank next. Debts are paid by the head son. Widows go to the heir, who sacrifices a goat to the dead man.

At Edelu the rule is the same, but the widows go to the father's brother if the son is small, and the brother buys another wife for the son when he grows up.

At Idumibo the head son takes the property, and may at will give to his brothers or father's brothers. The father's brothers are the next heirs, and they give a share at will to the grown daughters. Widows go to the eldest son. The father's brother is guardian for the youthful heir and feeds him till he grows. If there is any property left when the son attains manhood he can claim it; if not, there is no palaver.

At Ako the rule is the same, but all daughters get shares if there are no sons. The father's brother is apparently not bound to hand over the property to a son when he reaches manhood, but only " gives him things." A son is considered old enough to inherit at fourteen or fifteen.

At Uromi the head son collects all the property and takes his share, the remainder goes to his father's brothers. If the head son is small a father's brother comes to look after the house; the boy can claim the whole of the property, but the guardian may use it; he can also take the wives and buy others for the son. Failing sons the king takes all, and even the daughters get nothing; the father's brother takes no wives, but the price for a daughter is paid to him. He also takes the house, but the farms go to the king.

At Ubiaja the head son is the heir, and his father's brother is his guardian if he is small; the guardian may retain goats and cloths, but not cows; he may take the big wives, and the small ones have friends till the son is grown up. If a man has no heirs the king takes his property, and he is buried by the quarter. If a man has no sons he may make a daughter arhewa in some places, but this is not the custom in Ubiaja.

At Auči the widows are divided first and go to the amoiya sons if there are more than one widow, to the brother of the deceased if there is only one, for a son cannot marry his own mother. According to one statement the eldest brother of the deceased takes the first share of the rest of the property; but it appears that it goes in reality to the sons in order of age, and to the brothers only if some remains over. The daughters get cloth, beads, and goats. Farms go to the head son, but the brothers may get a share of them and agree to work with the head son or separately. If the sons are small, the brother takes the children and the property as guardian, but does not seem bound to account for what he has received.

The children of the isomi wife remain in the house of the father and belong to the brother or son (in amoiya); the heir gets dowry for the daughters given in isomi or amoiya.

At Uzaitui the head son of an amoiya wife is the chief heir, and the other adult sons of amoiya wives get shares, which are settled by an old man. An isemi wife's son does not take property unless he elects to remain in his father's country. If there are no adult sons the brother of the deceased takes and keeps the property; the next heir to him is the head of the family. The son of an isemi wife can succeed if his father makes him a chief or, according to one authority, if he buys him from his mother's family. The son of a daughter by an amoiya wife, herself married in amoiya, is also a possible heir.

An isomi wife's son may take from his mother's brother.

A puzzling case came under observation here. The son of an isomi wife inherited from his mother's brother; later he moved from the house thus obtained to his own father's house, of which he was said to be the real owner, but shared it with the son in amoiya of his father's own brother in amoiya.

At Fuga, and probably as a general rule in this part of the Kukuruku country, a man's heir is either his brother or his brother's son or his own son, whichever is the eldest. This kind of succession is known in " pidgin English " by the convenient term " big and big." Adult daughters get no share even in the absence of sons. As before, an isomi wife's son may take his father's property: (a) if his father makes him a chief; (b) if he elects to stay in his father's country; but a condition of succession for the sons of both amoiya and isomi wives is that they shall have joined otu.

The son of an isomi wife takes from his own brother, from the son of another isomi wife, from the son of a sister married in isomi, from the brother of his mother by an isomi marriage, or of his father by the same, from a brother by the same isomi mother, from the mother's brother's son by an isomi marriage, or the mother's sister's son, from his mother's mother, from the son in amoiya of a brother by an isomi mother, and from the son of his father's sister by an isomi marriage.

Here, too, was a case which I failed to elucidate. The husband of an isomi wife was stated to have taken a house from her at her death, which her son afterwards inherited from him.

At Fuga if a man has a daughter by an isomi wife he takes the bride price. If the father is dead it goes to his brother, and in either case the mother takes half. Formerly,

F

when Nupe people made raids the father and the wife's
father divided the daughters between them. If a child were
sold in amoiya and the father did not get a share of the
bride price, his wife's family would be compelled to give him
another child. That is to say, if out of four daughters one
was sold in amoiya the father takes two and the wife's
family one of the remainder.

At Yanipodi I obtained the following details as to
inheritance, without, however, being able to check them by
reference to genealogies.

The children of an isomi wife take property from the
mother's brother if his own sons in amoiya are small, and
vice versâ his amoiya son is the heir if the sister's son dies ;
but if the sister's son's son in amoiya is the elder, he is the
heir.

In the Ibie country of Northern Nigeria the heir is the
eldest son of an isogo or enabọ wife, failing a son the
eldest daughter. The next heir is the eldest brother or
brother's son (big and big) or sister or sister's son (do.).

At Kominio the eldest son of an enabọ or onawateva
wife takes the property; the ateme widows go to the own
brother of the dead man, and he receives dowry for them
from their eventual husbands. An enabọ wife goes to a
brother by an enabọ wife. Old widows go to the house of
their fathers or mothers. Failing a son the eldest daughter
succeeds, and the next heir is the deceased's brother.

The children of the ateme wife do not inherit from the
father but from the mother's brother if he has no enabọ
child.

At Igiawe a son is a woman's first heir; a daughter can
only obtain property through her father, who ranks next to
a son. At Ewu the daughter is entitled to a share, but the
husband claims the rest. At Edelu the son takes, failing him
the husband, who claims even what the woman brought from
home.

At Idumibo the son succeeds if he is old enough ; if not,
the father takes all except woman's things, which go to the

daughter. The husband gives some of the property to the wife, who takes charge of the boy. At Ako the son only takes if he is adult.

At Uromi the head son takes, failing sons the woman is iyeye, king's mother.[1] A woman may own trees, cattle, slaves, etc.

At Ubiaja a woman can own or take care of a house in addition, but in that case she cannot marry; freedom of choice is left to her.

A woman's property descends in many different ways in the Kukuruku country, if the statements made to me are reliable. At Auči the children take their mother's property whether she is isomi or amoiya; in the latter case the husband is the next heir, in the former the elder sister, or one of the family; there appears to be some formality which compels the son to take the property to his mother's family in the first instance and then receive it back from them.

At Uzaitui, according to one statement, the property of a woman goes to her son, failing a son to a daughter and failing her to the head woman of her compound.

At Fuga a woman's property goes to an adult son or daughter or to a sister by the same mother, or to the mother's sister.

At Agenigbodi the brother of an isemi wife has preference over the son, who takes from the mother's brother. An amoiya wife's property goes to the other amoiya wives of the same husband or to his brother's wives.

In Soso half of the movables go to the eldest child, male or female, if adult, the other half to own brothers of the dead man; the child takes the house. If the child is small its share is kept for it. Debts are payable by the brother in any case, and the brother might be seized, if the child were pawned or seized, and substituted for it.

If there is no child, brothers and sisters share the property. The goats and some of the cows and half the farm go to the child; oil palms bought by the deceased go to the brother;

[1] See p. 89.

F 2

those inherited are divided. The same rule applies to bought and inherited land; it should be noted that the son takes all the land if the own brother is dead but has left children, and if one of the sons is dead, the inheritance goes to the other sons and to his children *per capita, i.e.*, equally.

At Semolika the head son gets a big share, the rest take equally; the mother acts as guardian to small children. The sons can agree to give a small share to the brother of the dead man. Failing sons the own brother succeeds, the next heirs are the father and mother (?); then the gravediggers and the mother's family.

At Ibilo property is divided equally among sons and daughters and the head son takes a big share. The mother can act as guardian, but may apparently dispose of the property freely if she likes. The dowry of a daughter is payable to an own brother of the dead man, who must share with the family. If one of the sons is dead, his brothers and descendants inherit *per stirpes, i.e.*, by families.

At Irua a woman may own trees or slaves as well as the ordinary kinds of property held by a woman. At her death the eldest son or daughter inherits, failing them the husband, in which case the family of the woman reclaim slaves or cows; finally the king steps in.

At Sugbenu, near Irua, a woman might own these classes of property and her head son is the heir; failing a son, the daughter takes a share and the rest goes to the brothers of the deceased; things made in the husband's house are his property.

At Yanipodi the amoiya wife's property goes to her children; failing them to another amoiya wife; failing her to her husband's sister. In the case of an isemi wife the children succeed, failing them the brother or his children.

At Kominio a woman's property goes to the eldest child; failing children to an own brother or sister; the next heir is the mother's brother or sister. The rule is the same at Soso : women cannot inherit trees, but may buy them. At

Semolika a woman's property goes to her children equally. At Ibilo the children and brothers share.

A posthumous child at Irua gets no share of the property, but belongs to the second husband of his mother, and ranks before all subsequent children in questions of inheritance. The same is the rule at Igiawe, but he does not rank as heir; the second husband buys him a wife.

At Uromi and Ubiaja he passes to the second husband with the property. The same is the case at Yanipodi.

At Semolika a posthumous child takes a share of the property and the mother is the guardian, but she cannot be called to account.

At Irua the real father retains an illegitimate child if the girl is not betrothed; if the child goes to the mother's husband it ranks according to age for a share in the property. The rule is the same at Ewu and Fuga.

I was told at Yanipodi that the same rule applied even to the child of a girl sold later as amoiya wife.

At Okwoloho in the Sobo country the eldest child of each wife gets a share, the head son takes most. In one case the eldest son took three goats, two widows, twenty cases of gin, one slave, all the cloth (£3) and yams together with the house; one daughter took two goats, one cocoanut, one slave, five cases of gin and £3 in cowries; another got £3 in cowries; and a son got some fish poison.

One of the widows had previously married the dead man's deceased brother and might not marry anyone else in the family.

At Eferun the rule is the same, but the father's brothers also share.

The partition in one family was as follows:—

I eldest son; II second son; III and IV father's own brothers; V and VI sons.

	I.	II.	III.	IV.	V.	VI.
Widow	1	1	1	1	—	—
Slaves	2	1	—	—	—	—
Goats	2	1	—	—	—	—
Plantain trees	all	—	—	—	—	—
House	1	—	—	—	—	—
Cocoanut trees	2	1	—	—	—	—
Cloth ... ...pieces	15	10	5	—	—	—
Gin ... ... cases	20	8	—	—	1	1
Yams	20	10	—	—	5	—

At Ajeyubi the property goes to the head son and the brothers of the deceased; other sons get a small share; a daughter cannot rank as a son, but the head of the family will give her a present. The own brother of the deceased is guardian, but is not responsible for stolen or lost property. If he uses money in trading, some goes to the guardian, some is treated as interest and goes to the heir.

At Ugeli the eldest sons of each wife, or failing them the eldest daughters, take the property and the head of the family divides it. The brother gets a small share. If there is only one wife she goes to the brother. The brother and mother share the dowry for a daughter.

The brother is the guardian, failing him the head of the house or the mother. The guardian is not responsible for loss of the property if he has not enough to cover his debt; the inheritance is not handed over in full till the son is married.

A small share of the mother's brother's property comes to the children.

At Ewu the head son gets two widows, eldest head sons of other wives one; ten cases of gin go to the head son, five to the second, three to the others. The house goes to the head son. After these shares have been taken the eldest brother gets five, the other three or four cases of gin; a daughter gets five pieces of cloth and a case of gin, unless she is the eldest, when she gets ten cases of gin. All sons and all daughters get some share of the property.

At Ugo near Ewu the head son gets one widow and seven cases of gin, the eldest sons one widow each and four or five cases, the small sons one case each. The head son takes the trees, and the small sons divide the yams. The daughters get equal shares of cloth with an extra share for the head daughter. A sister's son gets one case of gin.

At Evleni the head child gets all the property. The deceased's own brother is guardian and takes the wives if the heir is not an adult male. If there are four wives, two would go to the head son, one to the father's family, one to the mother's family.

At Owe the head son takes all, but a brother gets a widow; one or two go to the father's family, none to the mother's family.

At Iyede the head son is the heir, but gives shares to his brothers, and may give them widows also. If the eldest child is a daughter she gets a big share, and the eldest son takes the remainder. If there are no sons or brothers a daughter can take the house and land.

At Agbasa the head son is the heir, and if there is plenty of property he will share it out to his brothers and uncles on both sides. If there are only daughters, the eldest takes all and retains it at marriage. A woman can take the house, but if a brother of the deceased is near he claims it. He acts as guardian to a small boy and takes the big wives.

At Kokori the head son gets a big share, the other children take equally, and one of the widows will go to the father's family. The next heir is the deceased's own brother. A daughter may take the house, but must hand over land when she gets a husband.

At Okpara the head son takes all and the others get presents from him; daughters get a goat. A brother receives a small share and acts as guardian.

At Ovu it is incumbent on the head son to share the property out, though he is nominally the heir; the brother receives a share. Failing sons, daughters succeed, but take neither house nor land if they are married.

The deceased's brothers or the mother are guardians; yams are sold, other food shared ; goats may be sold or kept. A man does not inherit from his mother's family.

At Jesse, in the Kwale country, the head son takes all, but "dashes" the small children ; he takes three widows, one goes to the deceased's brother, one to the head of the family, if there are enough. If there are no sons the head daughter takes all and dashes her sisters ; house and land pass to the deceased's brother when the daughter marries, but she can retain trees.

At Sapele the head son gets a big share, the others take equally; the deceased's brother acts as guardian. Daughters get such things as cloth, pots, calabashes, beads, and goats, and may get cocoanut trees if they are numerous.

At Warrifi the head son gets a big share, other children small shares, but a brother takes the house if they are only daughters. Widows are shared out in seven days, the remainder of the property at any time.

At Amukpe the head son or daughter succeeds, and other children get small shares ; if there are only daughters the brother takes the house, but a daughter can return to it if she leaves her husband; a daughter may take a farm and retain it after her marriage.

At Okwoloho the eldest son takes a big share of a woman's property, which goes back to her family if there are no children. The rule is the same at Eferun, and the elder brother of the father divides the inheritance. At Ajeyubi the husband takes if there are no children, but at Ugeli he has no claim. At Ewu and Ugo the rule is the same as at Eferun, but at Evleni the eldest child takes the property. At Owe the children share equally ; at Iyede the eldest child takes, and even what a woman makes in her husband's house goes back to her family.

In Agbasa all children take equally. The same is the rule at Kokori, Ovu, and Jesse. At Amukpe the eldest takes a big share.

Posthumous children are usually treated like other children

in the Sobo country; this is the case at Evleni, Iyede, Aghasa. I was told that they take nothing at Ugo. At Ugeli and Ewu, on the other hand, the Šekri rule seems to have influenced the custom, and the " last child " (ublevie) gets a big share in the same way as the eldest.

At Kokori it does not share, but inherits if it is the only child and the mother's second husband is the guardian.

At Okpara the deceased's brother is the guardian and the crops go to the mother; of course the second husband is frequently the brother, and the rule is therefore identical with that of Okpara.

The illegitimate child of a woman, whether before or after marriage, gets no share of the husband's property.

At Ugo a child by a friend before marriage gets no share of its father's property, but this information was contradicted by another informant, who said that a child by a " friend " would get a share and rank as son, according to relative ages. At Evleni, Agabasa, Kokori, and Okpara this is the case.

ADOPTION.—Among the Edo-speaking peoples adoption seems to be practised only within very narrow limits. I found a fair number of cases in which a man was either unmarried or had no children; in none of them could I discover that steps had been taken to adopt a child, even where there were no other relatives and no heirs of the same family. In Edo itself, women with property would adopt the king and be termed iyeye; the king would bury her and take her property.

A childless man is apparently free to adopt a child with the consent of its parents, and the child will bury him, but it does not take over his awa, unless it is a slave and put as priest to worship him. If there are no children such a child may take the property. If there are other children it may get a share of the property, but must behave well to the other children.

The head of a house may take any child as his own, others only children by the same mother, and this subject to the claim of the head of the house. He may adopt a daughter and give her to a chief as a wife; in this case the chief buries him and takes all his property.

An adopted son would sacrifice to his own father as well. The king takes the property of an heirless man.

In Ijeba a woman may make the king her heir and he buries her; but if she has a brother he has a prior claim. At Aroko brother's or sister's sons may be adopted and live with adopted parents; failing sons, daughters have the preference.

In the kingdom of Agbede adoption is mainly or entirely penal, that is to say, if one man kills another his family pay two persons to the family that has lost the man, and the adopted persons become full members of the new family, with the same marriage restrictions and the same duties of sacrifice; if the dead man was an eldest son, the newcomer takes his place as heir.

In Irua, on the other hand, penal adoption is unknown, but a childless man may purchase an heir, even if he has brothers to succeed him.

At Jagbe a boy or girl may be bought and adopted, but they do not take over the full duties of a child, for they would sacrifice only to the man who adopted them, but not to his wife.

At Fuga a childless man can buy an heir who will take his property and sacrifice to his new father; the child may not marry either into the old or the new family.

If a man is killed, either the culprit or another has to be paid to the family as compensation; he sleeps under the shed for seven days; uwoko, a root like koko yam, is dug for him to eat, and he must also consume the head of a rat and of a hen.

In the present day a man is sent to court and the blood custom cannot be carried out, for it involves the payment of a person; this means that there will be another "accident," for the palaver is not at an end.

At Yanipodi the adopted person enters the new family and may not marry into their original family, though the children are allowed to do so. They are heirs only in the absence of adult brothers of the deceased ; they get no property from their original family.

In the Uzaitui country penal adoption is practised ; the adopted son sacrifices to his own and his new father and mother, but he will take property from the new family only. If the father of small children is killed the adopted person takes the property and the children.

PROPERTY.—*Land.*—In theory, the whole of the land of the kingdom of Edo belonged to the king, and all the people were his slaves. There were, however, certain differences between landlords in Edo itself and those recognised in the villages. The inhabitants of the city claimed the right to hunt anywhere in the kingdom, but permission had to be asked by a stranger who wished to hunt on village land. A settler in the village obtains his farm and land for his house by application to the headman of the village. In the city, however, all land appears to have been paid for, and no length of possession would give a title to an intruder.

The boundaries of village or other land were marked by means of trees, and there was a class of officials whose duty it was to decide disputes.

It is difficult to ascertain how far prescription was recognised. Probably the customs differ from village to village. New villages were occasionally founded, and settled by permission on land claimed by other villages. It does not appear that the grantor village could expel the grantees, and after a certain length of time the land appears to have changed hands. That is to say, the grantees would themselves be in a position to become grantors. If, as sometimes happens, a village disappears entirely, the land appears to be appropriated by the nearest village. Where land is begged from a village for making farms, the users pay first fruits to the lenders, but the grant appears to be perpetual.

In connection with grants of land for farms, it must be remembered that the native system of cultivation is not intensive. A farm is cultivated for one year, and produces yams ; in the second year women may cultivate, and produce pepper, beans, and the like; then it lies fallow for a period of years. Each village has, therefore, far more land than it requires at any one time for farming.

In the Edo country property in land does not exist, so far as individuals are concerned. Land cannot be granted to an outsider, except by the head of the community, save that it is possible for an individual who has made a farm and is leaving the village to hand the farm over to a friend who will care for it.

Occasionally farms are worked in common, but, as a rule, if a large farm is made for protection against wild animals, the ground is marked out; occasionally, however, two or more brothers will cultivate a farm in common, and will draw on the yams as occasion demands.

Occasionally too, after the death of a man, his farms are worked in common until the produce is ready.

Natives are apparently free to build houses where they choose; a stranger has to ask permission. A house once built is personal property; it cannot, however, be sold, and if a stranger leaves the village his house reverts to the headman, who again can only hand it to another occupant.

It happens not infrequently that a house is broken down owing to the poverty of the family or other causes; the worship of the ancestors appears to be kept up in such cases, and to constitute an effective assertion of the right of property.

In Okpe I was informed by the king that he was the owner of the land, but his rights appeared to be restricted, for I was told that a house could be built anywhere without leave, even by a stranger. If a family becomes extinct the house is derelict, and is called afogbo. Anyone may take possession.

At Otua, an Ichimi tree marks the boundary of the village land. A stranger must ask permission before he makes the farm, and land can neither be sold nor pledged.

At Idegun, the customs of the Ida districts seem to have influenced the landlords; I was told that a native marks out his plot by blazing the trees before he clears it, and that he may give it to another man at will.

At Ekpe, near Irua, leave need not be asked to make a farm, but a stranger asks permission before he builds a house. If he leaves the village, his property in it is transferred to the man with whom he lodged before the house was built.

At Fuga, there appears to be more personal property in a farm, for a man makes it where he will, and can give both it and his house away; anyone may take possession of a deserted house.

In the Uzaitui country the chiefs of Ikbe and Apasiu lay claim to all the land, but since the Hausa invasions, people have given up asking leave to make farms.

In Auči the land is vested in the king and the chiefs, and all men ask leave before they make their farms, which they begin on the same day.

In Yanipodi there are five compounds, but all the village land is vested in the oldest man. Each farmer brings him a tribute of from five to ten yams annually.

In Soso each quarter has its own land, which is vested in the headman, though individuals have their own plots. Properly speaking, the consent of the quarter would be required before the land could be sold by the headman, but if the headman chooses to disregard this rule, there appear to be no means of compelling him to share the proceeds with the community, and no means of revoking the sale.

In Semolika farms and land are hereditary, and fathers and sons appear to work their land in common. Land may be lent, but the arrangement must be renewed annually. There is also common land, which passes into possession of the man who first cultivates it.

In all the country with which we have hitherto been dealing, selling or pawning of land is absolutely unknown. In a few cases it is vested in individual families, but such cases are exceptional. In the Sobo country, on the other hand, each family owns a portion of the village land, and as in the remainder of the Edo-speaking territories, a portion of this land is each year selected for cultivation. Each family appears to clear a large plot in common, but each owner can show his own small plot.

Where there is insufficient land in a given family the sons may, as a rule, claim land for cultivation from their mother's family, and permission may not be refused. If this family, too, has no land to spare, application may be made to another family; but in this case the grant is optional, and permission must sometimes be purchased.

At Okwoloho the fee for permission may be as much as three pounds, but for use in following years there is no payment. The lessee, however, is bound to give them the option of taking one of his daughters as a wife, subject to the payment of the usual dowry. If the marriage takes place, and a son is born, the land in question becomes his property. Unmarried sons frequently cultivate in common, but they divide the produce before it is gathered.

At Eferun the payment for use of land for one year is two shillings in the case of a townsman, but a stranger is said to get land from his hosts for nothing. Here, and probably elsewhere, in addition to the family land, there is communal village land, permission to cultivate which is given by the head of the town. The head of the family gives permission to a stranger to build a house. The fee is two pounds for the first year, one pound for the later years. Land round a house is inherited by the eldest son, and he grants small portions for houses to his brothers.

In Iyede the head of the family grants land to his brothers for one year, and where the land is insufficient further grant may be obtained from the chief. At Agbasa and Kokori, and other places, farms may be sold. At Okpara a woman cannot inherit land if she is married, but a widow is not similarly barred. If she dies without marrying again the land is said to pass to her children, but I was unable to verify this statement.

As a rule, hunting is free to all, but the headman of the town sometimes lays claim to a fore-leg of the animal, and there were certain regulations as to how the carcase of an elephant was to be divided. One of the tusks was the property of the king.

Trees.—Regulations in regard to property in trees are exceedingly various. In the Edo country, in the king's time, the Iroko tree was royal property. Other trees were only claimed as property where the products were useful. There was no property in trees, now used for their wood alone, such as mahogany.

In the greater part of the Edo-speaking territory the oil palm is common property. At Otua, Auči, and Ikbe some are common, others individual property. In the Sobo country they are in the main individual property, but there are a few exceptions. Next to the oil palm, the most important trees are cocoanut and kola, and these are almost invariably private property.

The number of trees which produce fruit is inconsiderable : in addition to kola and cocoanut, native orange and mango, native rice, lime, and paw-paw almost exhaust the lists of uncultivated products. The only other trees claimed as private property are those which produce leaves for making soup, those which produce substances used for marking the body, and those which produce rope.

In the Edo country, and sometimes in other parts, kola or other trees found growing wild in the bush may be claimed by the discoverer, who clears a small space round the tree. Where a farm is made round the tree thus claimed the owner of the tree has the right of access.

At Ugo anyone who finds a kola tree in the bush must enquire if it has an owner. If no owner is found, the discoverer shares the property in it with the ogie.

At Usen kola found in the bush cannot be made private property. If a kola tree stands in the farm of another, the farmer picks the nuts and shares the produce.

As a rule, women are not permitted to own kola or cocoanut trees; if they plant them, the property is usually vested in a male relative.

At Ijeba anyone who finds a fruit tree in the bush claims it by making a clearing and putting medicine on it.

At Aroko a stone is sometimes put in the fork of a tree, as a sign that someone has claimed it. At Okpe oil palms are common property, but only natives are permitted to take nuts from them. At Otwa, on the other hand, oil palms planted by individuals are private property. I was told that all oil palms had owners formerly, but that they are now common property, except in so far as claims dating back to the period of individual ownership can be established.

At Idua, oil palms appear to be privately owned, at any rate, when they stand in a farm, for the farmer can forbid access.

At Awoiki a farmer is permitted to make his farm round another man's kola tree, but he must do so with care, and permit access.

At Ako and Idelu, ownership in trees cannot be set up by clearing the bush, and the same is the case at Fuga. An oil palm there is common property in the open; private property in a garden.

At Apasiu, the headman claims the oil palms in the village, those outside are common. As a rule, the trees which bear the fruits used for marking the body are common property; but at Apasiu this right is limited by the right of the farmer to exclude trespassers.

At Kominio, Ogba, the leaves of which are used for soup, grows wild. When they burn the grass, a clearing is made round such a tree by the owner. A new tree may be claimed as the seedling of the old one.

At Semolika where the land is private property, the ownership of oil palms goes with the land.

In all this country the selling of trees is practically unknown, and it is only rarely that pawning is permitted.

In the Sobo country the law relating to trees is, like that which relates to land, one which gives far greater freedom to the individual. Generally speaking, trees may be either pawned or sold. As a rule, the owner of land claims all trees growing upon it, unless he has granted permission to plant.

Where land and trees are in different hands, access may be claimed at any time, subject to a small payment being given. An oil palm in the bush growing outside the limit of family land may be claimed by the finder. Limes and paw-paws appear to belong to the whole town.

At Ewu, if a cocoanut grows on a farm that is leased to another person, the farmer takes the produce of it, but this right appears to be limited by the right of the owner to grant permission to a third person to plant.

The rule that only males may own trees is found sometimes in the Sobo country; occasionally, as at Okpara, cocoanuts may not be sold, or, as at Agbasa, kola; while at Ovu there appears to be a general prohibition against selling trees.

Water.—It is a singular thing that over nearly the whole of the Edo territory the only villages in the neighbourhood of water are those inhabited by Šekri, or other alien races. In some cases villages are no less than six miles from the water side, and in the dry season practically the whole of the water has to be carried this distance.

Under the circumstances, it is not surprising that fishing is not normally an occupation of the Edo tribe. As a rule, their supplies are drawn from the Šekri. Only in the Sobo country and the north-eastern portion of the Edo territory, do we normally find property in stretches of water or fish swamps. Rights in these are hereditary, and descend to the eldest son. Fish fences are set up in the rivers, but apparently there is seldom or never any recognition of individual rights to stretches of water.

In the Sobo country, and occasionally elsewhere, wells are found which are the property of the various quarters. If however, a private individual digs a well, he has no exclusive claim to its use, and anyone who notifies him, that he desires to draw water from it, is at liberty to do so.

Pledging, Loans, and Debt.—In the kingdom of Edo, and in other parts of the country, it was the custom to pledge the children, or other members of the family, for debt. Human beings were not precisely sold into slavery in this way, for it was a recognised thing that, on payment of the debt, they were free. Except in the Sobo country, pledging of land was not usually permitted, and not always there. Pledging of trees[1] was commoner than pledging of land, but was not invariably permitted. As a rule, the seizure of pawns for debt or as security for a runaway wife was not permitted in the market. In some places an unlimited right of seizure existed, the result was that there was no market.

I got a most detailed account of the customs connected with pledging at Fuga. Only human beings and movable property could be pledged or seized; for a debt of one pound, a person; for two shillings, a goat; and the pawn might be any person belonging to the country of the debtor. It was the duty of the debtor to set the pledge free; if he had no money, however, the pledge might be sold, or the owner of the pledge, if he had one, might redeem him and recoup himself by seizing the actual debtor. If a pledge were sold, he could be redeemed by his own family with two persons, one goat and five shillings. Anyone who seized a pledge might be himself seized by the man's family; but the pledge who escaped apparently gained his freedom. If, however, the pledge ran, another person could be seized in payment. If a woman was pledged, the holder might marry her; but he would rarely do so, if she were so near home that she could run away. He could, however, take another person in her place, if she ran, and retain any children. If the debtor found the money, a woman who had been pledged and married was free, but not her children; if, however, the children ran, they were free.

The regulations as to loans appear to be somewhat indefinite. Length of time has apparently little or no influence on the interest payable. Interest is not necessarily expected, though it may be offered as an inducement by a borrower who is anxious to get money.

At Otwa no interest would be paid unless agreed upon before hand, but it might amount to forty per cent. on the

---

[1] For the customs as to trees, see p. 95, ante.

principal for a loan of six months, though the period has no influence on the total interest payable.

At Idua no interest is paid on a loan.

At Fuga there is no interest on a loan to a friend, but forty per cent. may be charged in the case of a stranger.

At Ajeyubi, in the Sobo country, interest is payable at the rate of about twenty per cent. for an unlimited time. When the lender wanted his money back, it would be borrowed elsewhere.

At Ugeli interest is not paid on a loan, but a day is fixed for repayment. If payment is not made up to time, interest, or rather damages, at the rate of about ten per cent may be claimed.

The recovery of loans is virtually the same thing as the recovery of debts.

At Agbede and a few other places, the host of a stranger who dies in debt may be made liable for his debt.

At Uromi a man may seize a goat or gun for a debt, or, if it is a big one, even the person himself might formerly be seized, or yams which are already stacked. A debt due from one person may be transferred to another in satisfaction of a claim. This is also the case at Fuga.

Money lent is recovered by the same process as an ordinary debt; it is proved by the evidence of witnesses. A creditor who dies will tell his son, and in former days sasswood might be employed as proof of the evidence. If a debtor dies far from home his creditors take his body to his family and claim the money. The body is buried by the family, and payment of the debt cannot be asked till it is buried.

At Uzaitui, if a man had been seized and died, he was thrown into the bush; no one buried him, and the debt was extinguished.

In the Ibie country the host gets the property of a stranger who dies in his house, but he is also responsible for his debts.

At Kominio, if one man owed money to another and did

not pay his debt, some of his people could be seized and sold, unless they were redeemed in five days.

In the Sobo country, as already noted, the rules about pawning are somewhat different.

At Agbasa trees, houses, or land are pawned for one year only, but, as repeated pawnings are permitted, the practical result of this regulation is small. Formerly children could be pawned for three years, after which they could return, even if the money was not paid.

At Ajeyubi a creditor could go three times to the debtor and demand payment, then seize some of the family and hold them. As soon as the debtor met the claim the pawns were free. A debtor might pawn his children after formal consultation with the mother.

At Ugeli, when a man dies in debt, his sons have to pay— if necessary, by borrowing. Failing sons, a brother is responsible. The property is divided before the debt is paid, and then all members of the family make contributions. In default of payment, a child or other person might formerly be seized; but permission would be asked of the head of the family, and if he declined to pay the debt, permission had to be granted.

As noted elsewhere, property may be given in charge to another man with or without payment for his services, the amount varying. The caretaker is sometimes responsible for a stolen object, but as a rule is free from responsibility if animals die. At Fuga, if goats are given in charge, the care-taker can dry them, if they die, and send them to the owner. If they are stolen the caretaker must apprise the owner, in which case he is free, even if they were stolen by his default.

There was a certain distinction in the kingdom of Edo between the slave of the house and the bought slave. If the slave of the house was given to the daughter, and the daughter bore no child, the slave went back to the old family. If a slave of the house was given to the king's wife, he always stayed with the king and became ovioba, which practically meant that he is free, for all chiefs and all free men were termed o v i o b a—slaves of the king. These o v i o b a established the king's villages, together with the slaves that were bought with the king's own money.

At Gwaton acquired slaves were such persons as prisoners in war, persons sold for debt, or criminals. A slave could run from his master to the king, and a woman slave could run away and call herself the king's wife. Slaves' farms belonged to the master at their death, but their produce was the property of the slaves.

Edeki was the slaves' day for working on their farms, and morning and evening of ordinary days. A female slave might be married, and if she were the child of a slave belonging to the same master her father became free. Such a wife was technically free, but did not occupy quite the same position as an ordinary wife.

At Idua in the Agbede country the slaves were acquired in the same way. A prisoner of war would be free when he escaped. A slave of the house was not sold except for crime. The family of a female slave who had married her master were thereby set free.

At Ikbe in the Uzaitui country, if a man were sold as a slave, his wife and children could go to his brother and were no longer his. A slave might marry either a free woman or a slave. Slavery was individual, and the children are free. His family might redeem him, or in some parts of the country he might even redeem himself.

At Eferun the child of a male slave and a free woman was free, but the child of a slave woman and a free man was a slave. If a man married his slave the children were free. The father of a slave wife was not free, but the rule as to his position varied in different parts of the country.

At Iyede the status of a child was determined by the status of the mother when it was born, but a master who married a slave thereby set her free. Slaves remained slaves and could not accumulate property, but they might be redeemed. If a man were sold as a slave his property belonged to the seller, as also did his wife and children. Of course where the property, including the family, was worth more than the debt, some arrangement would always be made. If the father of a slave died, the slave's share of his inheritance went to the master.

SECTION V.

LAW.

IT is a cardinal principle in native African law that the commission of a crime sets up a relation of debtor and creditor, save in such cases as the offence which is regarded as God palaver, and is punishable by death.

Among the Edo-speaking people, few, if any, offences came within the latter category, but other crimes besides murder were punished by death in Edo itself, for which elsewhere a milder sentence was substituted; this was owing to the fact that human sacrifice was prevalent, and there was a great demand for victims at a cheap rate. Details of some of the sacrifices will be found elsewhere.

Murder.—In addition to murder, homicide was also recognised, and, if this explanation was put forward, enquiry was made as to whether there had been a previous quarrel between the parties.

At Ijeba, a murderer was hanged in the market-place, and, in case of homicide, a substitute is handed over to the family.

At Okpe and Otua the only punishment of murder was the cost of purchasing of the substitute. Accidental or justifiable homicide was not punished.

At Ewori, however, homicide of all sorts and murder are punished in the same way—by the fine of one person against the injured family.

At Uzia the family of a murdered man were at liberty to burn the house of a murderer and seize his farm. Over and above this, there was a fine of one person. Justifiable homicide was not recognised unless a man acted in self-defence at a distance from the town. In the town, a man who was assaulted by another was expected to summon assistance.

At Agbede a murderer was handed over to the family of the deceased, and they were at liberty to kill him, sell him, or accept him as a member of the family. Only in cases of homicide was the offender permitted to substitute another person.

In the Ishan country the family does not appear to have received compensation, the fine was payable either to the king or to the community as a whole.

At Fuga two persons were paid to the family of the deceased. At Ikpe, in the Uzaitui country, if a murderer were put to death he was hung upon a tree. His family were permitted to cut him down and bury him if they paid a goat to the community.

In some places the penalty was the same, even if the murderer were a member of the same compound as the murdered man.

In Ikbe, however, if the murderer were of the same compound, he would not be killed, but the belief was that he would die within a year, for the ghost of the murdered man would come and kill him. The murderer would see the murdered man coming with his cutlass on the farm road, or when he sat down to eat the murdered man would appear before him and hinder him from eating.

At Agenigbodi all the people went to the farm of a murderer and destroyed his property, they could go to his house also and break it down, and destroy or take away the household property. Then the murderer would be driven into the bush for two months, after which he had to return and make certain payments. In the first instance one shilling and sixpence, in order to have the ashes of the burnt house swept up, and one shilling and sixpence for water to drink, after which he could drink where he liked. Then a sheep was caught and killed, and the murderer had to pay for it. Two persons and four shillings were paid to the family of the deceased, and when they were handed over the chiefs and all the people were present.

At Yanipodi a murderer would be killed if he did not belong to the same compound as the deceased; otherwise, two persons would be paid. These persons joined the family of the dead man, and could not marry back into their original families, though their children were allowed to do so.

At Kominio summary punishment might be inflicted, but if the murderer escaped to the bush, two thousand four hundred cowries were given to the chief, and two thensand four hundred to the mother of the murdered man. After nine days, the two families met the chiefs and old men and women and the case was considered, after which a substitute had to be paid to the family of the murdered man.

At Soso a murderer used to be sold to the Beda people; his family might also provide a substitute, and in that case the murderer knocked his head against him and handed him over.

At Semolika a murderer was killed and no substitutes were allowed.

At Ibilo a murderer was driven out, but his wives and children remained. His property was divided, and his wives were free to marry.

In the Sobo country, at Okwoloho, a murderer would hang himself; if he ran away his farm would be destroyed, and also the property of his father and mother.

At Eferun the murderer was compelled to hang himself; if he ran away the family of the dead man burnt his house and drove his family out. If the murderer were not found, one member of his family had to hang himself in the next three years, or a fine of three persons was payable to the family of the dead man.

At Ugeli the murderer hanged himself to the beam of his house, if the murdered man were a member of his own town. If he were a stranger, the two places would fight with one another.

At Ewu war between the families was the result of homicide. They were at liberty to fire guns at one another, and there was no punishment if anyone was killed.

At Iyede a murderer was hanged by the brother of the dead man, who subsequently offered plantains to the executed prisoner. As an alternative to this, a murderer might be dragged with a rope along the ground till he died, but in this case, the brother of the dead man took no part.

Theft.—The punishment for theft varied within wide limits. In some places, if the matter did not come before the chiefs, restitution and payment of expenses was all that was required from the offender. In other places a thief was sold into slavery, or even killed.

In Edo itself a thief's hands were tied behind his back, and he was flogged round the town. In the villages the punishment was less drastic.

In Usen a thief was taken round the town and laughed at by everyone. He was compelled to return the stolen object, but there was no further punishment. A stranger was, however, flogged in addition, and he would be imprisoned until a fine was paid.

In Ijeba the stolen object had to be restored, and a fine of ten shillings was paid. If a goat had been stolen and eaten, two goats had to be repaid, and a fine of ten shillings was also payable.

At Sabongida a fine of twenty-eight shillings was payable to the chiefs, and in default of payment the thief might be executed.

At Idegun a thief who came in the night might be killed. If the theft were committed in the day, the thief was caught and kept till his family redeemed him by a payment of four pounds. The punishment was in somes places, to a certain extent, within the choice of the injured party.

At Ewori, in the kingdom of Agbede, the thief was tied up till the property was restored, and the owner was at liberty to sell him or let him go as he pleased. In all this part of the country theft in the market, which in some parts of

Africa is severely punished, is regarded as a trivial offence, because detection is so easy. At Ijeba the fine was about one penny.

At Otua there was no punishment at all. It is a common practice to put goats or other property in charge of a relative or other townsman ; if such a goat were stolen, the holder of the goat had to name the thief, otherwise he was responsible for the value.

At Uzia a thief, if he was seen, paid the value of the stolen article and a fine of two or three pounds. If he was a stranger the townsmen at Uzia were at liberty to go to his town and kill goats, and the offender was responsible for their value. Theft in the market-place was punished by confiscation ; if the thief was a stranger, a man of the same country simply restored the property.

At Woriki, in case of theft, the suspected family or quarter could be called upon to take an oath. If they took the oath no further legal steps could be taken. A known thief could be accused on circumstantial evidence. If anyone was shown to be present when a theft was committed, he was held responsible for anything lost or stolen unless he could name the thief.

At Eda a thief had to restore the property and pay a fine of two pounds to the whole town, some of which went to the chiefs, some to the owner of the property.

At Fuga theft might be punished capitally, or the offender might be sold as a slave. Theft in the market was punished by imprisonment, and a fine of one pound.

If an Ikpe man went into the Hausa country and was sold in punishment for theft, the Hausa who stole at Ikpe could also be sold.

At Yanipodi a man who stole in the market simply restored the stolen property. There is said to be a night society, whose object is to prevent theft, but whether they are not sometimes responsible for the disappearance of stolen property seems an open question.

In the Ibie country theft was punishable by the sale of

the offender into slavery. The family might also be made responsible.

Goats might be killed to the value of several pounds, and the thief was responsible to the losers. Even if a thief were killed in the act, the property might be destroyed and compensation would be payable.

At Kominio, if a householder were killed in the struggle with a thief, there would be a trial by ordeal. Theft was punished by selling the offender, but if the theft were in the market this penalty was only carried out in the case of old offenders. At Soso the punishment of theft was a fine, but when a man stole from a farm, it was assumed that he must have been hungry, and only a light punishment would be inflicted.

At Semolika a thief would be tied up with a rope, and his family would have to come and ransom him, the amount payable being proportional to the value of the object and the circumstances under which it was stolen. If a thief came at night and were killed, the householder put the stolen object upon the chest of the dead man and allowed the corpse to lie till morning.

In the Sobo country complaints are universal that cases of theft are far more numerous now than in the old days. At the present time the punishment is a comparatively light one, but in the old days the penalty was far more severe, and the fine was substantial. In some cases the offender was put to death, in others there was a money penalty up to ten or twelve pounds. A thief caught in the act might be shot without penalty.

At Ajeyubi complaint was made in case of theft to the head of the club. A meeting was called, and the chief had to restore the goods and pay a fine of ten or twelve pounds.

In the theft of plantains the fine was two pounds, and for theft in the market two shillings only.

At Evleni a thief was sold, whether the property stolen was valuable or not.

At Iyede theft from the house or market was punishable by hanging the offender.

Assault.—Penalty for assault differed considerably, and in many cases the penalty varied according to whether an attack was made with a weapon or without one.

At Ijeba, common assault and wounding were punished with a fine of one and ninepence; for a second offence the fine was five or ten shillings.

At Uzia anyone who committed an assault in the town was punished by having his goats seized.

At Fuga punishment was inflicted only if there was a wound.

At Auči there was a fine of six shillings for an assault with cutlasses. If a stranger were attacked, the fine was payable to his hosts, and he shared it with his guest.

At Ajeyubi, in the Sobo country, a man who was wounded by another showed the wound to the head of his family, whereupon the two families went to war, and fought all day till three or four had been wounded on each side. Then the case was regarded as settled.

Assaults upon women seem to have been rare, and punishment for them rarer still.

At Ijeba, I was told, that a man who assaulted a girl would have his house destroyed.

At Otua one goat and eight shillings was payable to the chief for such an offence. But such attacks must have been extremely unusual.

Arson.—In many places arson seems to have been unknown as an offence. Where it was known, the payment of the value was in some cases sufficient to expiate the offence; in others, it was regarded as an act of war.

Abuse.—The only other offence known to native law seems to have been abuse. Comparatively heavy penalties were inflicted upon those who called a man a slave, or otherwise took away his good name.

Ordeal.—If a crime has been committed and the culprit is unknown, or if a person is suspected of a crime, there are various methods used by the natives to discover the truth. In the first place the help of supernatural powers may be invoked, and accused people may be compelled to swear that they are innocent. It is believed if they swear falsely they will fall sick. If it is impossible to make this appeal to the supernatural, the person who has had property stolen, or who has been otherwise injured, may himself go to a shrine and invoke vengeance upon the wrong-deer. Or he may, according to the native term, " bring out the Ebọ to find the thief." This is done usually by taking the emblems of Ake and carrying them along a road, ringing a bell at the same time. The person whose property has been stolen calls upon Ake to punish the thief if he does not deliver up the goods. Where a person or body of persons is suspected the Ita ordeal is the commonest. This consists in passing a fowl's feather halfway through the tongue of a suspected person, and repeating words to the effect that if they are guilty may Ita stay in their tongue, whereas if they are innocent it may come out. This trial is made three times, and guilt or innocence pronounced for accordingly. Where the problem is to select a thief from the houses of a given quarter, each house sends one representative to the trial, and the house selected by Ita is then put on its trial and its members proved individually.

Another form of Ita used especially in the Sobo country is to pass a nail through the ear. If the man is guilty the nail passes through, if he is innocent it breaks. A third form is to use plaited leaves and decide upon the guilt or innocence by whether they can be unplaited or not.

Trial by fire is also known; it is said that a calabash of burning oil is placed upon the heads of the suspected persons.

In another form, medicines and a cowry are put into a pot of palm oil; the accused has to pick the cowry out: if he is innocent, the fire goes down; if he is guilty, a big flame follows him and burns him.

A third form of ordeal by fire is found in the Sobo country, where an axe blade is put in the fire, and suspected persons wash their hands in medicine and try to pick out the axe.

For witchcraft, and occasionally for other crimes, the sass-wood ordeal was the recognised procedure. Large numbers of persons must undoubtedly have lost their lives, for in a recent case at least eighty met their death in this way. It was the custom, if any one member of a family was selected by the sass-wood, for the remainder to suffer death with him.

If an accusation was made, and a sass-wood ordeal resorted to, the accuser had to pay one person to the accused if the ordeal resulted in a declaration of his innocence.

SECTION VI.

KINSHIP.

THERE are two systems of indicating kinship, by which we mean relationships traceable by genealogy. One of these, the descriptive, is mainly used among the white races. the other, the classificatory, is confined to the coloured races of mankind. One form of the descriptive system is used among ourselves : relationships are indicated in it by terms showing the number of steps between the individuals concerned and a common ancestor. Thus brother indicates that the common ancestor is one degree removed from both. " Uncle " and " nephew " that the common ancestor is one degree removed from one. two degrees removed from the other. " Cousin " that the common ancestor is two degrees removed from both for cousins german, three degrees for second cousins, and so on. Relationships in the direct ascending or descending line are indicated by appropriate terms.

In a system of this kind a certain number of terms do double duty or more. Thus " uncle " may be the mother's brother, or the father's brother. " Cousin " may be the child of the mother's brother or sister, or of the father's brother or sister. Consequently the system is not absolutely descriptive.

In another form of the descriptive system, which we may term the Semitic, this ambiguity is avoided ; this form of the descriptive system of relationship is the one at present in use among the Edo-speaking people.

It is probable that the descriptive system has taken the place of a classificatory system. Classificatory systems have been found at widely separated points in Africa, and a few words must therefore be said as to their characteristics. In a classificatory system relatives whom we class together, such as uncles or cousins, are usually sharply distinguished, while other relatives whom we distinguish may be included under a common term, which may even embrace a number of people whom we do not regard as relatives at all. Thus, to give an example of this system in one of its most extreme forms, where a community is divided into two exogamous moieties, a child may apply to all the men of one generation of his father's moiety the same term that he applies to his father.

As a rule, the classificatory system of relationship depends for its existence upon the duties which are incumbent upon certain of a man's relatives. In some communities a very important function falls upon the mother's brother, who wields far greater influence than the real father of the child. As soon as these duties or rights begin to fall into abeyance, the tendency is for the kinship terms associated with them to go out of use.

An example of the use of terms similar to that found in a classificatory system is discoverable among many of the Edo-speaking tribes, though it is not necessarily due to the former existence of the classificatory system. It frequently happens that the father's brother is known by the same name as the father. In addition to this, there is a common kinship term, such as ǫtẹme, among the Edo which may be applied to anyone in the family, and simply means "my relative."

By collecting information as to kinship by the genealogical method described in the Appendix to this Report, it is possible to define with exactness the meaning of terms for which our language has no equivalent.

Among the Edo-speaking peoples a simple system prevails, and their neighbours, the Yoruba and Ibo, have, so far as my investigations went, a similar system—that form of the descriptive kind which I have above termed Semitic. In certain places special terms are found for the father's or mother's brother, but as a rule all kinship terms are built up from the simple terms, of which a tabular list is here given.

KINSHIP I.—Father, mother, son, brother, husband, wife, relative.

	Edo.	Ora.	Aroko.	Otua.	Okpe.	Agbede.	Irua.
Father ...	erha	erha ...	erha ...	ita	ita ...	erha ...	aba.
Mother ...	iye	inyo ...	inyo ...	eye	ewe ...	inio ...	oo.
Child ...	owi (omo)	omi ...	owi ...	omi	omi ...	omi ...	omi, owi.
Brother ...	¹owirha ...	erokpa	omierha ...	erokpa ominita	oita ...	omirha ...	oviaba.
	²owiye ...	inyokpa	ominyo...	omine inyokpa	omewe ...	ominio ...	ovioo.
Husband ...	odafoñ ...	odo ...	ose, oani norho	irha oloka	itao ...	odo ...	odo.
Wife ...	ame	oha ...	ame, oa ...	orha	orha ...	aue ...	ame, oha.
Relative-in-law ...	orua ...	orue ...	orua ...	orue	orue ...	orua, oyasa	orua.
Relative ...	ǫte ...	omio ...	—	—	—	—	omio.

¹ By same father. ² By same mother.

	Fuga.	Kominio.	Uzaitui.	Ibie.	Soso.	Semolika.	Ibilo.	Isua.
Father	etau	ita	ita	ita	ita	ita	iža	aba.
Mother	uwo	uwo	inye	inyo	inye	aiye, afa	olo	oi.
Child	oi	ovii	omi	omi	omoni	obili, omo	omo	omo.
Brother	[1] oietau, [2] oiuwo	itogo, inyogo	oguita, oguinye	itogo, eliminye	ominita, otumase	oho, —	—, —	[1] obeva, [2] —
Husband	olo	norho	ugue, odo	ogue	osono, okpai	osolo	—	oiya.
Wife	olo	—	ugue	ogue	osa	orha	—	okue.
Relative-in-law	orua, oyasa	orua, oyasa	ogo	ogo	ogo	ogo	—	oria.
Relative	—	—	—	omoi	—	—	—	—

[1] By same father.   [2] By same mother.

H 2

	Ugeli.	Iyede.	Aghasa.	Kokori.	Okpara.	Ovu.	Warrifi.
Father ...	baba	baba	baba	baba	baba, ose	baba	ose.
Mother ...	nene	nene	nene, oni	nene	nene, oni	nene, oni	oni.
Child ...	omo	omo	omo	omo	omo	omo	omo.
Brother ...	omose [1], omoni [2]	omose, —	omose, omoni	omose, omoni	omose, —	omose, —	omose., —
Husband ...	osia	orhai	ošai	ošia	ošia	osai	—
Wife ...	aje	aie	aie	aie	aie	aie	axa.
Relative-in-law ...	ogo, osolo	ogo, osolo	ogo, osolo	ogo, osolo	ogo, osolo	ogo, osolo	ogo, osolo.
Relative ...	—	—	—	—	—	—	—

[1] By same father. [2] By same mother.

In order to show how the Edo-speaking peoples form their kinship terms those in use among the Edo proper are here given (in the forms explained in the Appendix, p. 151) with an analysis to show their literal meaning.

	English.	Edo.	Meaning.	Reciprocal.
1	Father	erha	... ...	owi.
2	Mother	iye	... ...	owi.
3	Brother (B.F.M.) ...	owirowiye ...	child of father, child of mother.	
4	„ (B.F.) ...	owirha ...	child of father.	
5	„ (B.M.) ..	owiye... ...	child of mother.	
6	Sister...	owiye (3, 4, or 5).		
7	Father's brother (B.F.)	owirerha ...	child of father's father or *owirha* of father.	owiowirha (child of *owirha*).
8	„ (B.M.)	owiyerha ...	*owiye* of father	owiowiye (child of *owiye*).
9	„ sister ...	owirerha, owiyerha ...	as for 7 or 8.	
10	Father's brother's wife (W.B.F.M.).	amowirerha ...	wife of 7 ...	owiowirodafe (child of husband's *owirha*).
11	Father's brother's wife (W.B.M.).	amowiyerha ...	wife of 8 ...	owiowiyodafe (child of husband's *owiye*).

	English.	Edo.		Meaning.		Reciprocal.
12	Father's sister's husband (S.F.).	odafowirerha...	...	husband of 9 (7)	...	orua (relative-in-law).
13	Father's sister's husband (S.M.).	odafowiyerha...	...	husband of 9 (8)	...	orua (relative-in-law).
14	Father's brother or sister's child.	owiowirerha or owiowiyerha.	...	child of 7 or 8.		
15	Mother's brother	owiriye / owiyiye	... / ...	*owirha* of mother / *owiye* of mother	}	as for 7, 8.
16	„ sister	owiriye. / owiyiye.				
17	Mother's brother's wife.	amowiriye / amowiyiye	... / ...	wife of 15 / wife of 15	}	as for 10.
18	Mother's sister's husband.	odafowiriye / odafowiyiye	... / ...	husband of 15 ..	}	owiowirawoxa (child of wife's *owirha, owiye*).
19	Mother's brother's or sister's child.	owiowiriye	...	child of 15.		

	English.	Edo.	Meaning.	Reciprocal.
20	Sister's son's wife, and so on.	amowiowirha, etc.	...	owiriyodafon.
21	Father's father	ererha erhamodede.	great father	eye.
22	,, mother	iyerha	...	eye.
23	Mother's father	eriye ...	...	eye.
24	,, mother	iyiye ... iyemodede.	great mother	eye.
25	Husband	odafon, odafe...	...	ame, awoxa.
26	,, wife	olueme	one who does what I do.	
27	Wife's father...	erawoxa	father of wife	odafowi (husband of daughter).
28	,, mother	iyawoxa	mother of wife	odafowi (husband of daughter).
29	Husband's father	erodafon	father of husband	amowi (wife of son).

	English.	Edo.	Meaning.	Reciprocal.
30	Husband's mother ...	iyodafon ...	mother of husband ...	odafowirha, orua (husband of 6 (4).
31	Wife's brother ...	owirawoxa, etc. ...	*owirha* of wife	odafowirha, orua (husband of 6 (4).
32	„ sister	owirawoxa, etc. ...		
33	Husband's brother ...	owirodafon ...	*owirha* of husband ...	amowirha (wife of *owirha*).
34	„ sister ...	owirodafon ...	... ...	amowirha (wife of *owirha*).
35	Wife's sister's husband.	odaforua ...	husband of *orua* (38).	
36	Husband's brother's wife.	amowirodafon ...	wife of husband's *owirha*.	
37	Relative	ote.		
38	Relative-in-law ...	orua.		

It will be noticed that in the above table there is no distinction between brothers and sisters ; if necessary okwia or oxwo are added, *i.e.*, male or female. It may be noted that it is common for an interpreter to translate owiye by sister, whether it means a man or a woman ; care is needed to make clear the distinction between mother's brother owirhiye and " mother-brother," *i.e.*, owiye. The only other point to be noticed is that one word ame is used for wife in referring to those of other people or in general conversation, while a special word, awoxa, meaning simply young person, is used by the husband, in composite terms, when he speaks of his wife. It may be added that oteme is often used in reference to a brother ; and amoteme may mean my brother's wife. The use of the general kinship term, where a more specialised one could be used, is common.

It is exceedingly difficult as a rule to ascertain the precise authority of the head of the house. In Edo I was told that traders, farmers and other members of a house work for the head of the house and have time for their own work. They are liable to be called upon to do work for the head of the house and the head of the house has to be consulted on such questions as the betrothal of daughters. In the villages, however, the head of the house was in many cases a wholly unimportant person. I found cases in which the head of the house was an old man, actually living in the village, but without wives and apparently without property. He seemed to have no authority. Where the head of the house is resident in a more or less distant part of the country, his very name is often unknown, and it is highly improbable that he has any share in directing the affairs of the nominal members of his family.

In pre-European days the head of the house, where he was an important chief, possibly possessed a good deal of authority, including the power of punishing his dependants. A complaint is made, by the older men almost universally, especially in the villages, that the power of the head of the house and the old men is diminishing, and that the young men **now** disregard their orders. This certainly seemed to me to be the case.

At Kominio in Northern Nigeria I was told that the head of the house could authorise or prevent betrothals at will. If he were poor the family would meet and do work for him, but they do not seem to be responsible for his debts during his lifetime. After his death the family would pay, not exactly under compulsion, but to prevent him from being abused. The creditors would demand payment in five days; if proof of the debt were demanded, they might take earth from the grave and put it in water and drink it.

At Ajeyubi in the Sobo country, I was told that the head of the house claimed obedience of the members of his house and would be consulted about the betrothal of a girl though he would get no share of the dowry.

A trader would give him tribute to the extent of thirty shillings or so. In the case where a boy has gone to work for a white man, the head of the house would expect to receive money, but apparently has no recognised claim, inasmuch as the custom is not provided for by native precedence.

APPENDIX A.

Linguistics.

FOR the collection of Vocabularies or native texts, two things are essential, one is, a certain amount of training of the ear, the other is an adequate system of transcription. The training of the ear cannot be wholly acquired in the field, but with diligent practice it is possible to make great advances in this respect. If this practical experience is supplemented by a brief course of training from a trained phonologist, it is possible to do excellent work.

Transcription.—As regards the system of transcription, the cardinal principles are, that each sound should have a sign peculiar to itself and that each sign should represent one and only one sound. In order to do this, it is necessary to use a certain number of additional marks known as diacritical signs, which are added to vowels or consonants in order to mark their precise quality. Their use is not absolutely essential, except for scientific purposes, and a recorder who is indisposed, or unable to make himself familiar with their use, may omit them. Conversely, their use in a dictionary or volume of texts, need not deter anyone from making use of such a book through fear of complexity. If, for scientific purposes, it is necessary to distinguish two or three different kinds of " r," the diacritical signs do not alter the fact that the consonant is and remains an " r."

As a consequence of the two rules, mentioned above, a certain number of consonants of the European alphabets are rendered unnecessary. C, q, and x of the English alphabet, are rendered by s or k, kw, and ks. Conversely, certain signs have to be introduced in order to express sounds for which, in our alphabet, we have no distinct sign, as for example, the soft " ch," in Scottish " loch," or the soft "ᵍ " in North German " Tag." A sign is also needed for " th," though this occurs comparatively rarely in other languages.

C is brought in again to indicate the " ch " sound in " church," and " j " is used to express the corresponding sounds in " judge." In order to make it clear that " c " is used with this value, it is necessary to add a diacritical mark, and the same is added to " ĵ," in view of the different values which are given to this letter in other European languages. " č " and " ĵ " are therefore written thus. Similarly, to express " sh " and " zh " " š " and " ž " are written with the same mark. For " ch " soft as in Scottish " loch," " x " is used and for the corresponding soft " g," a new sign y. For " th " the old English " s " is suggested—ſ.

The manuscript of the vocabulary should always contain the following information :—

 (*a*) Name of language.
 (*b*) By whom obtained.
 (*c*) Where obtained.
 (*d*) Name of tribe (if possible with sketch map); if more than one name is used (*e.g.*, by neighbours), record all names.
 (*e*) Name and tribe of informant.
 (*f*) Name and tribe of interpreter.
 (*g*) Language used by interpreter (if not the same as is recorded).
 (*h*) An indication of the system of transcription employed.

ORTHOGRAPHY.—The simplest rule to follow is to sound the vowels as in German or Italian, and the consonants (omitting c, q, and x) as in English, each letter being confined to the expression of a single sound. But as it is sometimes necessary to discriminate more closely between various sounds than our alphabet will allow, the following table is suggested as a uniform standard.

Sounds not provided for and expressed by new symbols

should in every case be accompanied by a sufficient explanation, and, if possible, a diagram showing the position of the lips, tongue, etc., in producing the sound.

A. VOWELS.

a (ā) as in *father*.

a̧ (ă) intermediate between *father* and *cat*.

e (ē)—*take*.

ȩ (e)—*there*.

ȩ (ĕ)—*let*.

e̥—*bird*.

e̥ (e)—*but*.

i (ī)—*see*.

i̧ (ĭ)—*it*.

o (ō)—*stone*.

o̧ (ȯ)—*ought*.

o̧ (ȯ)—*not*.

u (ü)—*rule*.

u̧ (ü)—*bull*.

ṳ (ü)—German *güte*.

u̥ (ü)—German *glück*.

o̤ (ȯ)—German *könig*.

ai̯—*line*.

au̯—*how*.

ei̯—

oi̯—*boy*.

In the system of vowel indication here proposed, diacritical marks are invariably placed under the letter, leaving the top free for (a) × to show stress or dynamic accent, and (b) ` ´ to show tone or musical accent, both of which *may* fall on the same syllable. In brackets are given the diacritical marks recommended for use by German anthropologists.

The vowel system here set out is far from complete; it is therefore desirable to show how it may be enlarged if necessary. The signs ˌ and ˳ are built up from . used by Lepsius as the mark of the modified o or e, and — or | ; if therefore a vowel intermediate between ȩ and ȩ is needed, it should be written e̠; if a longer sound than ȩ is needed (as in French être), it may be written e̱ ; the same applies to the remainder of the vowels, though only in the case of e and o will more signs be needed in ordinary cases.

Any of the vowels may be nasalised, which should be indicated by the sign ˜ *e.g.*, *da̧* pronounced like the French *dans*. The length of vowels should be marked as shown in the table. Never insert r or h merely to lengthen a vowel (as " Lardo " for " Lado " ; " Dunquah " for " Dunkya ") ; nor double a consonant after a vowel to indicate that it is short.

The accent, in words of more than one syllable, should be marked thus × as in Sŏkoto, Kătsena. It is sometimes important to mark secondary accent in long words; this may be done by °, *e.g.,* Constantinople (Kǫnstạntịnŏpẹl). Where two vowels come together it is sometimes simpler to mark the asyllabic vowel instead of the accented one; this is done thus; few (fịu). It is necessary to show whether a syllable is open or closed, *i.e.,* whether a consonant forms the end of one syllable or the beginning of the next; this may be done thus; tea-time (ti/tạim).

Musical intonation, which is often (as in the Ibo and Yoruba Languages) the only means of distinguishing words otherwise identical in sound, but differing in meaning, should be marked thus :—

Rising intonation ájá (Ibo = " earth ").
Falling intonation àjà (Ibo = " sacrifice ").

B. Consonants.

b = b in *bed.*
č = ch in *church.*
d = d in *dark.*
f = f in *field.*
g = hard g in *gold.*
h = h in *have.*
ǰ = j in *jewel.*
k = k in *key.*
l = l in *long.*
m = m in *man.*
n = n in *not.*
ṅ = ng in *ringer.*
p = p in *pay.*
r = r in *red.*
ṙ = Scots or German guttural r.
rᵛ = cerebral r (trilled).
s = s in *sea.*
ś = sh in *she.*

t = t in *ten.*
ʃ = th in *think.*
ʆ = th in *this.*
ş = th caused by filed teeth.
v = v in *vivid.*
w = w in *win.*
y = y in *yellow.*
z = z in *razor.*
ž = z in *azure.*
b, p = b and p sounded nearly like w, with closed glottis.
x = approximately equivalent to Scottish ch in *loch.*
γ = soft g in N. German *tag.*
f, v = bilabial f and v Spanish pronunciation of b.

For those who desire a more elaborate system of consonant indication, the following diacritical marks are suggested.

Speaking generally, we may distinguish three positions in which any given consonant may be pronounced; (*a*) a forward one, in advance of the normal; (*b*) the normal one; (*c*) a backward one behind the normal one. T for example may be pronounced between the teeth, with the tongue touching the teeth or with the tip of the tongue on the roof of the mouth behind the teeth. These three kinds of t are written thus: ṭ, t, ṭ.

Where two consonants come together, as in atsa, the word may be pronounced at-sa, or a-tsa; this should be indicated or the sign of affrication -- ť -- may be used as in č or ǰ. The field is far from being exhausted by these few hints; but a more elaborate system is needed only in comparatively few cases.

The method of using this system can best be shown by a practical example.

Igịfiẹmido ;   Ẹmigẹrhamẹme ;   ịnạieva ;
I-don't-miss-anything ;   Thing-does-not-touch-me ;   those two ;

Ẹmighẹramẹmẹ ọmudia   unugwọba ;   Igịfiẹmido ọmudia
Emigerhameme   stood up   in palace gate ;   Igifiemido   stood

nokẹdo ;   ọkwekẹwafiohabọ ;   ifẹmẹ ọwelẹmigẹrhamẹmẹ ;
on hill of Edo ;   there he took bow ;   arrow   hit Emigerhameme ;

ẹkanọrọlobọ ;   ọkwegwowo ;   Igịfiẹmido ọkwẹgade
bead was on his hand ;   it broke it ;   Igifiemido came (back)

ọgiseva ;   ọwokpialẹxi ;   ọwinoị.
when he got there ;   said he was a man ;   he said he did not miss.

-gifiẹmido. Ẹmigẹrhamẹmẹ   ọwokpialexi ;   ọwẹmirhamino ;
Emigerhameme   said he was a man ;   he said thing did not touch him ;

ọmanọreva ;   owuwạiva   okpiawaxi.
person who was there ;   said you two   you are men.

The English of the translation in phonetic transcription

runs as follows (minor niceties of vowel indication being disregarded, though the vowels in English are seldom pure).

Double consonants should never be written unless both are distinctly heard (as in the Italian *an-no*), or the sound is, at any rate, perceptibly prolonged.

Ai dont mɪs çnɪ∫ɪṅ, ∫ɪṅ dẹs nǫt tẹč mi, ∫oz tu; Emighẹramẽme stud ẹp ɪn∫e palẹs¹ get; Igɪfiemïdo stʉd ǫn hɪl ǫv Edo; ∫er hi tuk bo: arо¹ hɪt Emighẹramẽme; bid wǫz ǫn hɪz hand¹; ɪt brok ɪt; Igɪfiemïdo kem bak; whẹn hi gǫt ∫er, hi sẹd hi wǫz ǥ mau¹; hi sẹd hi dɪd nǫt mɪs, Emighẹramẽme sẹd hi wǫz ǥ man¹; hi sẹd ∫ɪṅ dɪd nǫt tẹč him; persẹn wǫz ∫er; Iṅ sẹd yu tu ar mẹn.

Collection of information.—Any appearance of impatience should be avoided. If there is any difficulty in getting a particular word or phrase, it is better to leave it for another opportunity and pass on to the next, than to worry the native by insisting. In many cases intelligent natives will of themselves point out and name objects, *e.g.*, parts of the body, articles in or about the hut, etc. Words so obtained are of greater value than those directly asked for. No question should be asked which can be answered by a mere "yes" or "no."

All entries should be frequently checked by questioning different natives at different times and places, and the words and phrases tested by use among people other than those who supplied them. Words and phrases not provided for in the Form should be recorded as occasion arises under the following headings:—

1. Give the Salutations in ordinary use, noting: (*a*) the meaning of the words in each case; (*b*) the occasions when, and persons to whom they are used.

2. All names of relatives not included in the above vocabulary, *e.g.*, brother, sister, mother's brother, father's brother,

¹ The *a* in these words is shorter than that indicated by a, but no special sign is suggested for it as it is rarely needed in practice.

mother's brother's son, etc. (avoid the terms "uncle," "cousin"). The best way to do this is to construct a genealogical table (facing p. 142), entering all the relatives of a given individual by name (indicating the sex in each case), and then finding out what term of relationship he applies to each and they to him. If possible, such a table should extend over three or more generations, and include connections by marriage. The birthplace of every individual should also be entered.

3. Ascertain whether there is any hunting or fishing language, or sacred language connected with religious ceremonies and known only to priests or magicians, and those initiated by them; also any special *song* language, used in secular or sacred songs. Are there any secret languages taught to young people when initiated into the tribal mysteries? Or to the members of particular confraternities?

4. Are there any indications of a difference between the language of men and of women? *e.g.*, any words peculiar to the latter (such as terms of relationship), any difference between the pronunciation of the two sexes?

5. Is there any system of symbolic messages: *e.g.*, by means of knotted cords—any marks used to indicate ownership— any language of signs—any code of signalling by means of drums, or the like? Any marks on walls, trees; in sand or earth, at cross roads, etc.?

6. Note whether any letters are habitually interchanged by people in the same tribe, *e.g.*, whether some pronounce the same word with l and others with r. Local differences of pronunciation should be noted, *e.g.*, do the people of different villages pronounce the same language differently? Can any difference in pronunciation be traced to artificial deformations, such as tooth chipping, the wearing of ornaments in either lip, or the like?

7. How many cardinal points are recognised, and how are they described? Have their names any meaning in the language as now used? What are the names of the months? And how many are reckoned to a year? Is there any division of time intermediate between the day and the

month ? If there is such a division, have the days composing it any names ?

8. Give a list of personal names borne by men (at least ten) and the same number by women. Are any names given to one sex only ? Have they an obvious significance, and, if not, are they (*a*) archaic, or (*b*) borrowed from some other language ?

9. Any varieties, or apparent irregularities in the formation of the plural should be noted with especial care. Do adjectives change in the plural or in other ways accord with nouns ?

10. If there is any opportunity for noting words other than are allowed for in the above form, they should be arranged under the following general headings :—

A. Names of persons, trades, professions, tribes, words connected with the tribe and its organisation.
B. Parts and activities of the body.
C. (*a*) Animals. (*b*) Plants. (*c*) Minerals.
D. Heavenly bodies, natural objects and phenomena, etc., articles of food, agriculture.
F. Articles of clothing, ornaments, industries.
G. Weapons, hunting, fishing, war.
H. Abstract ideas, expressions connected with number, time and place, mental and moral qualities.
L. Words connected with death and funeral observances, spirits, witchcraft, the unseen generally.

Words and Sentences for Translation.

1. Head.
2. Hair.
3. Eye.
   Two eyes.
4. Ears.
   Two ears.

5. Nose.
6. One tooth.
   Five teeth.
7. Tongue.
8. Neck.
9. Breast (woman's).
10. Heart.
11. Belly.
12. Back.
13. Arm.
14. Hand.
    Two hands.
15. Finger.
    Five fingers.
16. Finger nail.
17. Leg.
18. Knee.
19. Foot.
    Two feet.
20. Man (person).
    Ten people.
21. Man (not woman).
    Two men.
22. Woman.
    Two women.
23. Child.
24. Father.
25. Mother.
26. Slave.
27. Chief.
28. Friend.
29. Smith.
30. Doctor.
31. One finger.[1]
32. Two fingers.
33. Three   „

---

[1] Methods of counting on the fingers should be noted.

34. Four fingers.
35. Five   „
36. Six   „
37. Seven   „
38. Eight   „
39. Nine   „
40. Ten   „
41. Eleven „
42. Twelve „
43. Twenty „
44. A hundred fingers.
45. Two hundred   „
47. Sun.
48. Moon.
    Full moon.
    New moon.
49. Day.
    Morning.
    Night.
50. Rain.
51. Water.
52. Blood.
53. Fat.
54. Salt.
55. Stone.
56. Hill.
57. River.
58. Road.
59. House.[1]
    Two houses.
    Many houses.
    All the houses.
60. Roof.
61. Door.
62. Mat.

[1] Note whether different kinds of houses have different names, and whether any of these are foreign (imported) words.

63. Basket.[1]
64. Drum.
65. Pot.
66. Knife.
67. Spear.
68. Bow.
69. Arrow.
   Five arrows.
70. Gun.
71. War.
72. Meat (animal).
73. Elephant.
74. Buffalo.
75. Leopard.
76. Monkey.
77. Pig.
78. Goat.
79. Dog.
80. Bird.
   Feather.
81. Parrot.
82. Fowl.
83. Eggs.
   One egg.
84. Cock.
85. Serpent.
86. Frog.
87. Spider.
88. Fly.
89. Bee.
   Honey.
90. Tree.
   Ten trees.
91. Leaf.
92. Banana.
   Plantain.

[1] If several kinds in use, note name and description of each.

93. Maize.
94. Ground nut.
95. Oil.
96. The tall woman.
    The tall women.
97. Large dog.
98. Small dog.
99. The dog bites.
100. The dog bites me.
101. The dog which bit me
    yesterday.
102. I beat the dog.
103. The dog which I have
    beaten.
104. I see him.
    I see her.
    He sees you.
    He sees us.
    We see you (*pl.*).
    We see them.
105. Beautiful bird.
106. Slave.
    My slave.
    Thy slave.
    Our slave.
107. The chief's slave.
    His slave.
108. We see the slave.
    The slave was seen by
    them.
109. We call the slave.
110. The slave comes.
111. He came yesterday.
    He is coming to-day.
    He will come to-morrow.
112. The slaves go away.
113. Who is your chief ?

114. The two villages are making war on each other.
115. The sun rises.
The sun sets.
116. The man is eating.
117. The man is drinking.
118. The man is asleep.
119. I break the stick.
The stick is broken.
This stick cannot be broken.
Break this stick for me.
120. I have built a house.
121. My people have built their houses yonder.
122. What do you do every day ?
I work on my farm (in the fields).
123. I ám going away.
I am hoeing (cultivating).
I am going away to hoe.
I am going to my farm.
124. The woman comes.
She[1] comes.
The woman laughs.
The woman weeps.
125. I ask the woman.
126. Why do you laugh ?
127. Why do you cry ?
128. My child is dead.
129. It is not dead.
130. Are you ill ?
131. My children are ill.

[1] Ascertain if there is a distinct pronoun for the feminine.

132. Her child is better.
133. Yes. No.
134. A fine knife.
    Give me the knife.
    I give you the knife.
135. I am an European.
    You are a black man.[1]
    You are a —— (insert
    name of tribe).
136. Name. My name. Your
    name.
    What is your name ?
137. There is water in the
    gourd.
    The knife is on the stone.
    The fire is under the pot.
    The roof is over the
    hut.
138. You are good.
    This man is bad.
139. The paper is white.
    This thing is black.
    This thing is red.
140. This stone is heavy.
    That stone is not heavy.
141. I write.
    I give you the letter.
    Carry the letter to the
    town.
142. Go away.
    Come here.
143. Where is your house ?
144. My house is here.
    My house is there.
145. What have you to sell ?

[1] Ascertain if any designation of this sort, irrespective of tribe, is current among natives themselves.

146. I want to buy fish.
147. The fish which you bought is bad.
148. Where is the man who killed the elephant?
    He has killed many elephants.
    How many elephants were killed yesterday?
149. Tie this rope.
    Untie it.
    Make the boy untie the goat.
150. My brothers and I, we are going, but no one else.
    Brothers! Let us go and tell the chief.

Note.—This appendix is in the main the work of Miss Werner and Dr. Struck, and I take this opportunity of thanking them.

APPENDIX B.

GENEALOGIES AND KINSHIP.

IN order to collect reliable information on many subjects, it is necessary to have recourse to more concrete methods than question and answer. If, for example, it is desired to investigate the native law of inheritance, entirely misleading replies will be given in answer to the question, "Who gets a man's property when he dies?" When, for example, I put this question in the Ida district, the answer invariably was, "His son." When, however, I came to investigate inheritance in concrete cases, I found that this answer was far from being universally true. In the first place only the sons of Amoiya wives, together with such sons of Isomi wives as have been created chiefs by their father, or as have elected, after his death, to remain in his country, are eligible to succeed to his property. They are in no case eligible unless at the time the property is divided they have joined an Otu. In other words, they must have reached the age of twenty-five or thirty. Further, the property of brothers is shared among the descendants of all the brothers on a principle known in pidgin English as "big-and-big." That is to say, a man's property goes not to his eldest son, but to the eldest among his sons or brother's sons, provided that they are by an Amoiya wife. Otherwise, his sister's sons are his heirs. Over and above this distinctions may be drawn between various classes of property, such as that gained in trade and that inherited. It is impossible to investigate these complicated laws of inheritance by any abstract method.

The recognised way of dealing with problems of inheritance

and similar questions is to deal with them by the so-called genealogical methods, examples of which will be found from another area in the Cambridge University's reports on the " Torres Straits' Expedition."

The difference which exists or may exist between the kinship system in use among ourselves and that of the people to be investigated makes it desirable to use as few terms as possible. If possible the terms used in making enquiries about pedigrees should be limited to the following :— " father," " mother," " son," " daughter," " husband," " wife," and, if necessary, " brother " and " sister "; but for reasons set out in the section on " Kinship " the two latter terms may be ambiguous, and they should be avoided if possible.

Genealogies.—The following notes on taking genealogies should be read after the specimen genealogies (pp. 149, etc.) have been studied.

The first step in recording a genealogy is to enter the name of one's informant, male or female. Then enquire what was the name of his father, making it clear that what is required is the name of the real father. Then the name of the father's father may be enquired, together with a list of the father's brothers and sisters, alive and dead. It is necessary in a country where plurality of wives exists to distinguish the mothers in this case; but it will often be found that an informant cannot recall the names of all his grandfather's wives. In this case it is necessary to show which brothers and sisters were of the whole blood, and which were of the half blood. This can conveniently be done by either of two methods; after the name of a brother may be put distinguishing letters, such as B.F.M. (that is brother by the same father and mother), B.F. (brother by the same father), or B.M. (brother by the same mother), or alternately, a long line may be drawn in the genealogical tree between the name of the grandfather and that of the father, and brothers or sisters of the whole blood written across this line, those of the half blood to the left of it for the same father, to the right for the same mother. The names of the husbands or wives of the father's sisters and brothers, together with the names of all their descendants, must be recorded. To do so on the same page as the genealogy of the informant and of his brothers and sisters usually results in great confusion. The most convenient method is to append letters or numbers to the names of all the father's relatives, and to deal with them on another page, one by one. These letters or numbers can, of course, be made to show the relative ages of the persons in question.

It will rarely be possible, in the case of ordinary people, to trace the pedigree further back than the father's father. If, however, further information can be obtained, it should be noted, as it will certainly prove useful in checking genealogies from other informants.

The enquirer will then proceed to investigate the pedigree of his informant on his mother's side, and ascertain the names in precisely the same way as for the father's side. This done, he may proceed to enquire how many wives the father of his informant had, and record their names, together with those of their fathers and mothers, the locality from which they came (this should be noted in other cases also), and the names of their children and grandchildren, if there are any. It is particularly necessary to press for the names, both of deceased wives and children. Many children die in infancy, and it is well, after getting a list of children alive and dead, to make supplementary enquiries as a check upon the list. If the question is put, "How many of your children have died?" the informant will often mention a number higher than that which he has given in the list of names. If possible information should be obtained as to the age at which children die. Though native ideas of time are exceedingly vague, it will be possible to discover whether the children died in infancy, as small children, or at a later age.

The informant may next be asked how many wives he himself has, and details of their pedigrees and descendants recorded in the same way.

In order to make the genealogical record complete there

is usually much information to be added to the tables besides the details of pedigrees and localities mentioned above. If. for example, there are exogamous divisions, such as those mentioned above (p. 55) in connection with the Ida district, enquiry should be made as to the division to which each person belongs. The tabulated information (see Genealogy II) will then show, firstly, whether children reckon their descent in this matter from their fathers or mothers; it will also show whether the traditional marriage laws are strictly upheld or not. Again, if, as in the Edo country, each family has a forbidden animal or totem (see p. 61), it is desirable to enquire into this for the same reason. An additional advantage to this procedure is that it gives a clue by which it is possible to discover family relationships not recognised or mentioned by the informants. Again, if there is more than one form of marriage, such as Amoiya and Isomi, enquiry should be made in each case as to the kind of marriage. This is quite essential when the enquirer proposed to deal with the laws of inheritance.

It is necessary in the genealogies, to distinguish between males and females. This may conveniently be done by putting the names of males in capitals, or by appending to the names the ordinary zoological signs for male ($\male$), and female ($\female$).

The information to be obtained from genealogies is extremely various. In the first place, in matters relating to the regulation of marriage, it is possible in a comparatively short time, without knowledge of the language, and with inferior interpreters, to obtain more definite and exact knowledge than is possible without it, to a man who has lived many years among a tribe and has acquired a thorough knowledge of the language.

In the second place, it is possible to discover with the utmost exactness, the kinship terms and their meanings. As will be seen by a reference to the section on Kinship, these terms are often exceedingly difficult for a European to understand, inasmuch as they are not exactly translatable into a European language any more than European terms are exactly translatable into a native language.

In order to work out the kinship system from a genealogy, the informant on whose information the genealogy is based, must be asked to say what terms he applies to each person in the genealogy. This may be written down, either underneath the names in the pedigrees, or the names may be numbered and a separate list of kinship terms made. The latter system has the advantage of making it possible to see at a glance all the persons who apply a given kinship term to each other. This should also be made the subject of a definite question. With these kinship terms, should be noted at the same time, their reciprocals, that is to say, in noting the terms which A applies to B and C, the terms which B and C apply to A, must be asked for at the same time. They may be written down after the kinship terms already obtained, and enclosed in brackets to distinguish them.

The laws of inheritance may be studied in two ways through the genealogies. In the first place, the enquirer may note down precisely how the property of a given deceased person was distributed, or how, if the custom is adhered to, the property of any living person will be divided. On the other hand, he may, after gaining some idea of the customs, endeavour to work out for himself how the property of a given man would be divided according to native custom, and then question his informant, as to how far his assumptions are correct.

A great advantage of a genealogical method, in all cases, and especially in matters of inheritance, is that it enables the enquirer to test the accuracy of his witnesses. In putting questions of this concrete kind, the enquirer is putting himself on much the same level as his witnesses.

It is frequently asserted that the chief characteristic of the savage is, his readiness to tell you what he thinks you want to know, regardless whether the information thus supplied corresponds to the facts or not. This kind of answer implies, as a rule, that the witness does not understand the real meaning of the question put to him, nor yet the object of his questioner. He does, however, realise in all probability, that his questioner does not understand what he is talking about.

I have always found the genealogies given to me to be entirely reliable with very few exceptions. The same names appear twice or three times or even more, when a number of genealogies are collected, once for example, in the father's pedigree, once in the mother's pedigree, once in the wife's pedigree, and so on. It will be found that names are sometimes omitted; it will sometimes happen that there are apparent contradictions, though enquiry will show that they may be due to the fact that two or more names are applied to one person ; in one case, which came under my notice, a man was ignorant of the name by which his wife was known in her father's house, and the father was equally ignorant of the name by which she was known in her husband's quarter.

The information gained from the genealogies about laws of inheritance will usually suggest many points for further enquiry. Cases of joint ownership will almost certainly be discovered, and the causes to which it is due can then be investigated. Exceptions to laws apparently general may be found in small communities, thus: at Iguiximi, in the Edo country, I found one family in which a child was handed over to the mother's family. In dealing with marriage, and inheritance, this point had not been mentioned by my informants. So many questions arise as to the family to which a given person belongs, that information of this sort, based upon a genealogical record, is of especial importance.

It is extremely difficult, by any ordinary method, to obtain accurate information as to the proportions in the sexes, the number of children per family, the mortality, in infancy or otherwise, the number of wives per husband, the effect of polygyny on fecundity, and similar matters Provided the genealogies are obtained on sufficiently wide basis, these questions can be answered statistically.

In this connection, however, it is necessary to warn enquirers of possible errors. It is almost certain that the memories of the people are less trustworthy for the children of past generations. In the first place, those who died young, or before marriage, never attained the social importance of those who had offspring. In the second place, if the genealogies are being compiled from information supplied by a junior member of a family, it is highly probable that he will never have known some of the senior members. Proof of this is given in the Section on Demography (p. 15). In statistics therefore compiled for an older generation, or including people not actually resident in the village (*e.g.*, of women who have married away), allowance must be made for possible forgetfulness.

As a rule, the folk are exceedingly poor, and an enquiry as to the amount of property which they possess, will probably be extremely unfruitful. In many cases beyond one or two cloths per individual, household implements, farming tools, a few goats and fowls, and a certain number of cocoanut or kola trees, a villager possesses little, except the crops which he has raised (or is raising), or possibly the seed for the next crop. It is, however, desirable, for more than one reason, to record on a statistical basis, the economic products of a village. It is extremely easy to ask each man at the conclusion of his pedigree, whether he makes a farm, and if so, whether he works it single-handed, and how much it produces annually. I have never met with any reluctance to answer these questions, and information has often been volunteered, as to what would be done with the surplus, if any, and the prices that would be realised. With crops such as yams, the information is readily obtainable. Statistics as to corn, cassava, or palm oil, demand more patience, and would be less reliable.

To collect statistical information on a wide basis, by means of a genealogical method, demands much time. If, however, a few villages are enumerated, and the enumeration is checked by ascertaining the number of inhabitants per house, which may be enquired in the first instance of each householder, in connection with genealogies, and independently of other informants at a later period, it is possible to ascertain the number of inhabitants per house, and on this basis it should be possible, by means of a count of the houses, to ascertain with some accuracy the population of a village. This may be checked by obtaining lists of the adult men, and ascertaining how many are married. This information can usually be obtained from one or two informants in each quarter, and demands only a very short time.

The advent of the European has caused a considerable change in the native mode of life ; in the old days it was not possible to wander about the country as is done at the present day. At the present time, a large proportion of the young men appear to leave some villages to work on concessions. Genealogies afford the means for discovering to what extent this goes on. This movement of population is probably undermining the native social system ; for under normal circumstances the work of such emigrants is available for the good of the community ; it is by no means impossible that their absence on a large scale may raise up problems of importance in the near future.

There are certain sources of error in genealogies collected in other areas, which may be mentioned here, though they are little likely to operate in West Africa. In some parts of the world, there is a taboo on names of the dead, and where this is the custom, it is necessary to collect information secretly, and not from the families in question. In West Africa, however, it is comparatively rare for people of one family to be able to give information about people of another, and the men with special genealogical knowledge, who are available in Oceania, do not seem to exist here. Another possible source of error is the custom of adoption, which, however, as is shown on p. 89, is only practised within very narrow limits among the Edo-speaking peoples.

Much variation may be found between persons in the

K

accuracy with which they are able to give a genealogy; in some cases, I found men unable to remember the names of some, or all, of their wives; others could not recall the names of their children; others again, who lost their fathers or mothers at an early age, were ignorant of their names, and were naturally wholly unable to say anything about earlier generations.

Specimen genealogical tables are appended to show convenient methods of dealing with the material. Table I shows a typical genealogy of the Edo country; it is, however, impossible to collect it in the form here given; for the amount of space required for each member of a family with his descendants cannot be estimated. It is, therefore, best to collect the rough material as shown in I*c*, which also illustrates the method of enquiry into kinship terms.

In I*c* Otomagie is the informant and the first step was to ask the name of his father and mother; then the paternal grandfather and grandmother were noted (the kinship term and its reciprocal being in each case obtained at the same time). The next names to be noted were those of Otomagie's father's brothers and sisters; in order to show the precise relationship the names of brothers of full blood are written across the line joining father and grandfather, half-brothers being written to the left for the father, to the right for the mother; figures are prefixed to their names to show the order of birth, and reference letters are added, so that the descendants of the brothers can be given below; in this way each table is kept of manageable size. The same device is used in the main table (I) for the daughters, who have either left the village or entered another family by marriage; in the latter case the normal course, where a complete set of genealogies is collected, is to put the cross reference only though of course all details are collected in *each* family as a check upon the correctness of the information. This applies to the female line generally.

It is convenient to distinguish the men of a village by their social rank; accordingly letters and numbers are appended to their names to show whether they are *idion*, *igele*, or *ologai* and their order within the grade.

It is convenient for statistical purposes to indicate the ages at least of children; if the ordinary zoological signs ♂ and ♀ are adopted for male and female, these signs may be varied accordingly; thus a baby in arms may be shown thus: ♂̆; a child of two to eight, ♂ and so on.

In the main genealogy the names of both husbands of Akuse are given, but if they are of different families, they will normally appear on different tables, with a cross reference. When genealogies are collected on an extensive scale it is convenient to have means of checking and extending the scope; family relationships may be unknown or overlooked by the informant. It is therefore well to ask the name of the head of the family (and, if necessary, enquire into the rules by which the headship descends; *e.g.*, get the names of successive heads and enter them in the genealogies) and the *awaigbe* (see p. 61) of both males and females. Where there are several of the same name this latter item is a convenient means of identification; moreover the scientific interests of the facts, and especially of exceptions to general rules is considerable. A third appendix shows the annual output of yams. To investigate the rules of descent enquiry should be made (a) into the descent of the property of people already dead, and (b) into the probable distribution of the property of living people.

Table II shows the method of dealing with cases in which there are (*a*) intermarrying classes (Ego and Atzikia, see p. 55) and (*b*) two or more kinds of marriage (amoiya, isomi and enabo). In practice it is convenient to devote a special page to any case in which there are a number of wives.

Genealogy III shows the system of inheritance in the Ida District ("big and big"). Where there is more than one kind of marriage it is always necessary to enquire into the ownership of the children; even in the Edo country, where only one kind is found, there are occasional exceptions to the rule that children belong to the father; and these exceptions can only be discovered by strict genealogical method ; the native mind is prone to generalisation (and the saving of trouble) in giving information.

Where land or trees are privately owned, the genealogical method is the simplest way of investigating the descent. If the table for a given family is compiled, (*a*) enquiry into the history of the trees or farms will suggest new names and enlarge the genealogy, and (*b*) the enquirer can test his grasp of the principles of inheritance (here as elsewhere) by attempting to decide who is the right heir and then investigating the cause of his error, if any.

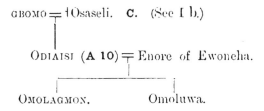

GBOMO ⚯ ₁Osaseli. **C.** (See I b.)

ODIAISI **(A 10)** ⚯ Enore of Ewoncha.

OMOLAGMON.   Omoluwa.

I, App. III.

Yams.
I, A 4[1] : 2 farms ; 7 ekbo from each.
I, A 9 : 2 ekbo.
I, A 11 : 2 ekbo.
A 10 : 2 ekbo.

[1] *I.e.*, Osagie (see main genealogy ; *cf.* p. 89).

GENEALOGY I.—IYAWA: (II) INOMINE QUARTER: *Oḅiaṣi.*

Males in Small Caps; females in Roman. † Shows that the person whose name is so marked is dead.

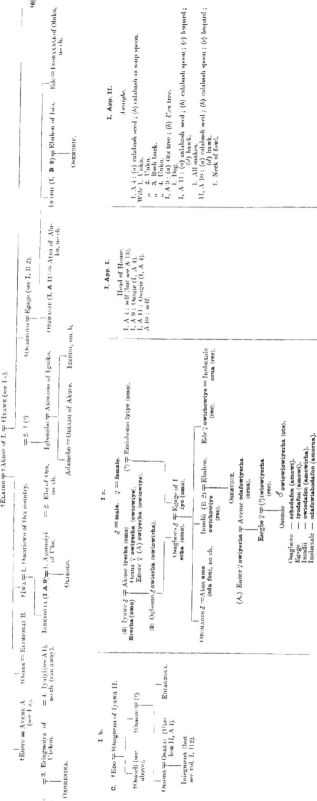

4.
İiodia.[1]

A.
⊤ 2. Oiyobo.
    Am.
    (see **OXOMI, 8.**)
no ch.

A.
⊤ 3. Akeeko.
    Is.

| *A.* | *A.* | *A.* |
| Окводu. | Ogomi. | Окwово. |

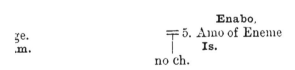

       Enabo,
ɟe.   ⊤ 5. Amo of Eneme
.m. | **Is.**
      no ch.

mily)

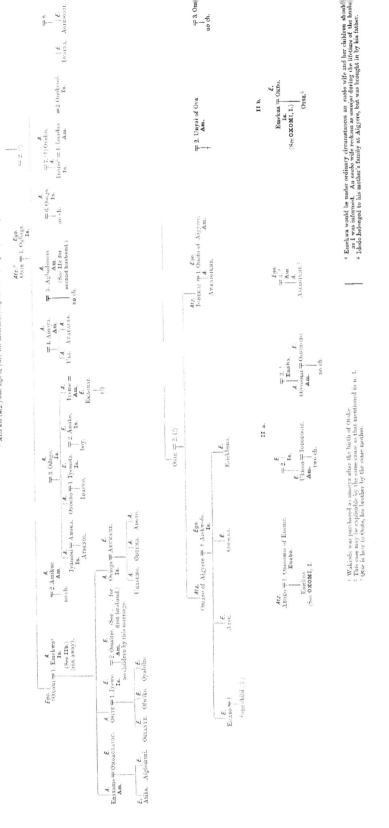

GENEALOGY II.—AGENEBODE: *Odi.*

* Atzi kin (Atz.) and Ego (E.) are the intermarrying divisions (see p. xi). Amoiya (Am.) doi Isoni (Is.)

[1] Enekwa would be under ordinary circumstances an *enobo* wife and her children should be, as I was informed. An *enobo* wife reckons as *amoiya* during the lifetime of the husband.

[2] Ihodo belonged to his mother's family at Aigrere, but was brought in by his father.

[3] Wakiedi was purchased as amoiya after the birth of Otile.

[4] This case may be explicable by the same cause as that mentioned in n. 1.

[5] Otse is heir to Osite, his brother by the same mother.

GENEALOGY III.—*Fuga*.

EBOSUA.

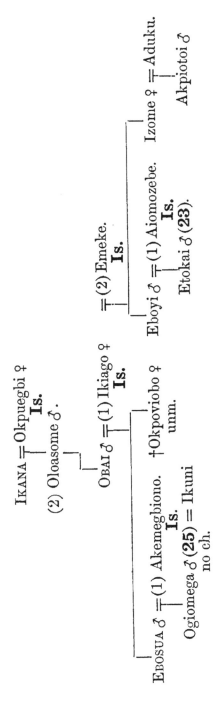

IKANA = Okpuegbi ♀
Is.
(2) Oloasome ♂.

OBAI ♂ = (1) Ikiago ♀
Is.
= (2) Emeke.
Is.

EBOSUA ♂ = (1) Akemegbiono.
Is.
†Okpoviobo ♀ umm.

Ogiomega ♂ (**25**) = Ikuni
no ch.

Eboyi ♂ = (1) Aiomozebe.
Is.
Izome ♀ = Aduku.

Etokai ♂ (**23**).

Akpiotoi ♂

Ebosua and Eboyi were made chiefs by Obai, and inherited his property ; Eboyi is Ebosua's heir ; when Ogiomega, who was made a chief by Ebosua, has joined *Otu*, he will be next heir to Eboyi.

Kinship.—It will seldom happen that all the kinship terms needed, of which a list will be found on p. 151, can be obtained from the genealogies. It is possible, however, to put hypothetical questions, based upon a genealogy, and in this way, to supplement the information.

In collecting the kinship terms, it is very desirable to exclude mistakes such as may arise from the possibility of a double relationship, or from misinterpretation ; if therefore they are available, it is desirable to question separately other people both men and women whose names appear in the genealogies, or, failing this, to collect three separate genealogies, with full sets of kinship terms.

Plurality of wives renders the kinship terms of West Africa unusually complicated. In all such relationships, as brother, sister, father's brother, father's sister, and terms based upon these relationships, it is necessary to enquire for three separate sets of kinship terms according to whether the relationship is whole or half blood, as explained above. In addition, there are frequently separate terms for older and younger brother. If these are included, six sets of terms will be obtained. It is possible that different terms may be used by men and by women. If these also are found to exist, twelve sets should be necessary, and so on. As a rule, kinship terms obtained from genealogies will be found to contain a personal pronoun. A will state his relationship to B, by saying B is " my father." Care must be taken, in compiling a list of kinship terms, to allow for this.

In enquiring for kinship terms by means of the genealogies, care must be taken to ascertain *all* the kinship terms that may be applied to a given person. It not infrequently happens that more than one kinship term is used for a definite relationship ; besides this, there is a general kinship term, meaning " relative," which will often be applied to anyone in a given genealogy, so far as the relationship is one of consanguinity.

Kinship terms to be collected are here given in the form of a table. In order to make sure that the information required has been completely gathered, it is convenient to have the copies of this list which can be filled up as the information is collected. For this purpose, it is only necessary to have a list of the terms on the left hand side, those on the other side being the reciprocals. The terms given in the list are sufficient for most purposes, but other terms are sometimes of interest and may be added. Among these are " father's father's brother " and " sister," with their children and grandchildren, and generally speaking any relationship for which an exceptional term is found, or the names for which seems to be unusual.

Term used by informant.	*Reciprocal used of informant.*
Father	Son.
	Daughter.
Mother	Son.
	Daughter.
Elder brother (M.S.[1]), B.F.M.[2]	*Younger brother.
„ „ „ B.F.[3]	
„ „ „ B.M.[4]	
*Elder sister (W.S.[5]) ...	*Younger sister.
*Sister (M.S.)	*Brother (W.S.).
*Father's brother	*Brother's child (M.S.).
* „ brother's wife ...	*Husband's brother's child.
* „ „ child.	
* „ sister	*Brother's child (W.S.).
* „ sister's husband ...	*Wife's brother's child.
* „ sister's child.	
*Mother's brother.	*Sister's child (M.S.).
* „ brother's wife ...	*Husband's sister's child.
* „ „ child.	
* „ sister	*Sister's child (W.S.).

* In the case of all these terms and their reciprocals it is necessary to find out whether there are different terms for B.F.M., B.F., and B.M.

[1] Man speaking.
[2] Brother by same father and mother.
[3] Brother by same father.   [4] Brother by same mother.
[5] Woman speaking.

Term used by informant.	*Reciprocal used of informant.*
*Mother's sister's husband ...	*Wife's sister's child.
* „ „ child.	
*Sister's son's wife (M.S.) ...	*Husband's mother's brother.
* „ „ child (M.S.)...	*Father's mother's brother.
⁻ „ daughter's husband (M.S.)	*Wife's mother's brother.
*Sister's daughter's child (M.S.)	*Mother's mother's brother.
Father's father	Son's son (M.S.).
„ mother	„ „ (W.S.).
Mother's father	Daughter's child (M.S.).
„ mother	„ „ (W.S.).
Husband	Wife.
Husband's wife.	
Wife's father	Daughter's husband (M.S.).
„ mother	„ „ (W.S.).
Husband's father	Son's wife (M.S.).
„ mother... ...	„ „ (W.S.).
*Wife's brother	*Sister's husband (M.S.).
* „ brother's wife ...	*Husband's sister's husband.
„ sister	*Sister's husband.
* „ sister's husband ...	Husband's sister's husband.
*Husband's brother ...	*Brother's wife (M.S.).
* „ sister	„ „ (W.S.).
Son's wife's parents ...	Daughter's husband's parents.
Father's wife	Husband's son.
Mother's husband	Wife's son.
Wife's father's sister ...	Brother's daughter's husband.
Relative.	

* In the case of all these terms and their reciprocals it is necessary to find out whether there are different terms for B.F.M., B.F., and B.M.

APPENDIX C.

PHOTOGRAPHIC AND PHONOGRAPHIC RECORDS.

IT is possible with comparatively little trouble, to collect by photographic means, a considerable amount of information of anthropological value. The material to be collected may be classified under the following heads : Physical Types, Arts and Crafts, Ceremonies, and Daily Life.

For Physical Types select typical adult males and females ; a few portraits of such persons should be taken, if possible, in characteristic poses, but not either exactly full face or in profile. Portraits of whole families provide exceedingly interesting material, provided the faces are sufficiently large. Further photographs may be taken of such details as tooth filing, face and body marks, body paint, abnormalities, and other points of interest.

For Physical types proper, it is necessary to photograph at least twelve male adults, and twelve female adults, in full face and profile, and if possible, a third photograph should be taken showing the top of the head.

It adds to the value of these photographs if the same persons are photographed at full length, with a scale of feet and inches at the same distance from the camera as the sitter. It is desirable to take subjects with closely cropped hair where it is possible, so as to show the shape of the head. Where the hair is abundant, it should be put back from the ear so as to show it fully.

If a background is used, light brown or French grey are the most convenient tints, and, if possible, the incidence of the light should be the same in every case.

It is most important to have an identification number or,

failing that, the name of the tribe and the sitter, in the picture. Where neither of these things is possible, as is often the case with head and shoulder portraits in a quarter-plate camera, a number should be written in pencil upon the gelatine, before packing it away or developing it. In all cases, a register should be kept of the photographs taken, and should include the number, or other identification marks, particulars of the subjects, the distance of the sitter from the camera, and the focal length of the lens.

As far as possible uniformity of scale should be preserved ; in no case should a portrait be so small that the distance from the top of the head to the bottom of the chin be less than one and a quarter inches. A convenient method of attaining uniformity, when once the size of the series has been determined on, is to regulate the distance of the subject from the camera, by the distance between the eyes and lips. The standard distance may be marked with lines upon the ground glass. A quarter plate camera is just too small to admit a head and shoulders portrait on the scale of one quarter, but with a good lens, a scale of one-fifth would be found convenient.

For the head and shoulders portraits, full face and profile, it will save much trouble to take all the full faces, then all the profiles. With a number of blocks of wood, it is possible to adjust the height of the sitter to a height previously marked on the background, so as to bring the head in the right place on the ground glass. It will save time if before he poses in front of the camera the sitter can take his place against the wall, on which a scale is marked, showing precisely what blocks are required.

For the profile portraits, it is comparatively simple, with some cameras, to get the exact profile. Where, however, it is proposed to take a considerable number with an ordinary snapshot camera, or in fact any other make except the Videx, a convenient method of securing that the sitter is in the right focal plane, is to set up a small mirror, so that the sitter can only see his face in it when he is properly posed ;

or a mirror may be set up at an angle of forty-five degrees to the sitter's line of sight, a cross painted on the mirror, and a pin fixed in front which the sitter has to keep sighted on the intersection of a cross. Probably, however, this latter method will be found too complicated for use with primitive peoples.

In dealing with Arts and Crafts, it is possible with comparatively little trouble to record all the details of a technological process, which can only be made clear with considerable difficulty by the use of words. It is convenient to watch the process first and take a certain number of notes, then the camera may be brought into use and each stage of the process photographed. Finally, the process may be watched a third time, points omitted in the original notes inserted, and the exact point noted at which the photographs have been taken. It is well to begin by taking a photograph of the scene of operations to show the craftsman and all his materials and tools. Then photographs on a larger scale may be taken to show the details of manufacture. It is often desirable to take a duplicate set in order to ensure the completeness of the series, in case of minor accidents to the plates.

An example of this method of illustrating technological processes, was published in " Man " of July, 1910, when I illustrated the methods of making pots in use in Southern Nigeria. The photographs actually published were less than one-third of the total number taken, and there was a further series illustrating the burning of the pots. The finished article should be photographed on as large a scale as possible, and a foot rule or other measure should be placed in the field to indicate the size of the object. Among the crafts which may be thus illustrated, are metal work, spinning and weaving, basketry, agricultural methods, palm oil making, fishing, carving of wood or calabashes, decorative art, and surgery.

It is naturally more difficult to photograph operations which are carried on under cover, but as a rule, the essential details of the procedure of weaving, or metal work, may be obtained by a few still-life photographs.

Such photographs duly labelled should explain themselves, but it is always desirable to send additional notes based on the observer's own information, and on information gained by enquiries.

Ceremonies are as a rule, either under cover, or attended by such masses of people, that photography is difficult. It is, however, frequently possible to get the chief actors to repeat the details, and, though it is not desirable to rely entirely upon photographs of ceremonies thus repeated for the benefit of the observer, it is an extremely useful method of securing details which may not come out in the original snapshots, and it has the additional advantage of permitting the observer to enquire into the details and meaning of the ceremonies at his leisure. If the chief actors are asked to explain the ceremonies, and are reminded of details by the enquirer's notes, taken during the actual ceremonies, they will often be willing to reproduce the whole thing exactly.

Nothing is more difficult than to describe in words the daily life of the people. The observer has to draw upon his memory in the absence of photographs for a mass of details which has to be sorted up and collated, and for such minor matters as characteristic attitudes and gestures, or the facial expression under the influence of various emotions, it is impossible to trust to memory. A systematic taking of photographs provides the observer with a ready-made index to his impressions, and they will contain points of interest which had not been noted at the time.

The most convenient form of camera is undoubtedly the Videx, fitted with a lens suited to all-round work. A telephoto lens may be of use, but of far more practical value is a front mirror which can be fitted at an angle of 45°, allowing photographs to be taken either to the right or the left. Subjects can then be taken at moments when they do not suspect the photographer of designs upon them, and all suspicion of posing is avoided.

Ordinary slides are not convenient for a long series of photographs; two or three dozen celluloid envelopes with a Mackenzie-Wishart slide, occupy far less space and are far more easily manipulated. They have the additional advantage that they can readily be loaded in the dark. For a series of photographs, if numbers coming within the field of the picture are not used, the numbers of the envelopes corresponding to the different photographs are noted at the time of exposure, and the current number of the negative written in pencil on the slide and transferred to the plates as above, when the changing is done.

A convenient method of dealing with the plates is to have consecutively numbered paper envelopes into which each is put, when it is taken from the slide. The details of the picture may either be noted upon this envelope, at the time of taking it, or a register of the ordinary kind may be kept, and the details transferred to the envelope afterwards. This method is, of course, chiefly useful when the plates are sent back to England to be developed.

A convenient aluminium box constructed to hold the camera and half a dozen or more plates, can be made to fit to the lamp bracket of a bicycle with straps to fasten it to the handle bar. By this means photographs can often be secured on the march when the camera would otherwise be inaccessible.

It is hoped that officers or private persons who already possess or who in the future take negatives of anthropological interest will forward copies to the Crown Agents for the Colonies, together with a list and any notes that can be given.

Each photograph should bear an identification number, and the name and address of the owner of the negative; the accompanying list should contain the name of the tribe, the subject, the date on which the photograph was taken, the identification number and the name and address of the owner of the negative.

Photographs will be registered with the British Association

and deposited at the Royal Anthropological Institute; access is permitted for purposes of study only, and applicants for permission to reproduce the photograph will be referred to the owner of the copyright.

Phonograph.—Valuable records of languages and music may be secured with the aid of a phonograph; for this purpose it is not necessary to use a large instrument; many of the best records in my possession have been taken with a small instrument weighing only a few pounds, and so small that it could readily be fitted into the aluminium box made to carry the camera on the bicycle.

For recording purposes, only a small horn is required; care should be taken that the mouth is kept opposite the centre, where a solo is being recorded. As a rule, a chorus is difficult to take down in the open air, as the sound is dissipated; but if the singers can be placed with their backs to a wall of rock, an effective record may be secured.

For musical purposes it is necessary to keep a record of the pitch, which varies with the speed of revolution of the phonograph. A pitch pipe should therefore be sounded into the phonograph before the melody begins, and at the same time, the date, tribe, and character of the piece should be recorded on the cylinder.

In taking records of music in which more than one instrument figures, it will often be necessary to move the performers or the instruments so as to take first one, and then another.

For linguistic purposes, it is essential to have a transscription and translation of the record, as well as the record itself. This is work which demands much patience, and two methods are available. The story may be taken down, and read out to the native a few words at a time for him to repeat into the phonograph. While he is not speaking, the phonograph may be stopped with the hand and restarted with a slight impetus the moment before the recitation begins again. With an intelligent native, it is possible to get a record which closely resembles the transcription, though they are seldom absolutely identical. The other method is, to take the record first, and then transcribe it, but it will be found that a native will seldom, or never, recall the exact words of his recitation, and that he will be unable to hear the phonographic reproduction, or if he does, that he invariably substitutes other words or varies his phraseology. These difficulties arise to a less extent if two intelligent natives are told to carry on a conversation; to record this two speaking tubes are more convenient than a single horn.

Where an observer has little or no practice in transcription, useful linguistic records may be taken by adopting the schedule of words and phrases printed in this volume, and getting a native to speak upon them successively into the phonograph.

INDEX.

Abuse, 109.
Adoption, 65, 70 76, 89 sq.
Adultery, 51, 54 56.
Agriculture, 16, 17, 36.
Ake, cult of, 30.
Akobie, 33.
Aluere, 32.
Amoiya wife, 54, 81.
Ancestors, 31, 37, 50, 78.
Animism, 27.
Arhewa, 79, 80.
Arson, 109.
Assault, 109.
Awaigbe, 41, 61, 141.
Awailimi, 61.
Awe, 27 sq.

Baskets, 22.
Birth, 29, 62.
Burial, 29, 40 sq., 53, 55, 99.

Calendar, 18.
Chieftainship, 13.
Child marriage, 57.
Clitoridectomy, 53.
Common property ; see Land,
    Trees, Water.
Cotton, 20.
Creation myth, 24.
Cults, 25, 30, 37.

Debt, 97.
Demography, 13.

Divorce, 54, 57.

Ebo, 25.
Edo kinship terms, 117 sq.
Ego and Atzikia, 55.
Errors in Genealogies, 14, 145.
Esu, 26, 32.
Exogamy, 55, 61.

Family, break up of, 61.
Farm, 91.
——— area of cassava, 17.
Fecundity, 15.
Figurines, burial, 44.
Fire, ordeal by, 110.
First-born, sex of, 15.
Food, 16.
Free love, 50.
Freedom of choice, girls, 50.
" Friendship," 50.
Future life, 25, 39.

Genealogies, 138 sq.
——— collected, 13.
Ghost, 27, 40.
Grammar, 8.
Guardian, 64, 68, 72, 75, 78, 79,
    84, 86.

Head of the house, 47, 49, 121,
    147.
Head-shaving, 45.
Homicide, 103.

House, 92 *sq.* ; *see* also under Inheritance.
Human Sacrifice, 35, 37.
Hunting, 91.
———— rites, 29.

Illegitimacy, 50, 51, 65, 76, 85, 89.
Impotence, 54.
Incest, 62.
Inheritance, 64 *sq.*
Initiation, 39.
Isomi wife, 54, 81.
Ita, 51, 110.

Joint ownership, 70, 75, 92, 93.

" King's mother," 89.
Kinship, 112 *sq.*, 117 *sq.*, 138 *sq.*, 150 *sq.*
———— terms, 114 *sq.*

Land, ownership of, 72, 75, 91 *sq.*
———— sale of, 93.
Language, 6.
———— secret, 38.
Languages, surrounding families, 6.
———— variety of, 5.
Last child, 89.
Liaison, 50.
Loan, 97.
Loom, 21.

Magic, 33.
Mamači, 44.
Market, 19.
Marriage, 47 *sq.*
———— prohibitions, 55, 61, 65, 90, 105.
Masks, 39.
Matrilineal descent, 55.
Matrilocal marriage, 59.
Mats, 22

Medicine, 25, 33.
Menstruation, 29.
Metal work, 23.
Morality, 50, 53.
Mortality, 15.
Mourning, 44, 45.
Murder, 103.

Neutral ground, 19.
Numerals, 10.

Obiame, 32.
Ochwaie, 32.
Ogun, 32.
Ohumewele, 33.
Olokun, 32.
Omeiho, 33.
Ordeal, 51, 109.
Osa, 24.
Osun, 32.
Otoñ, 41.
Otu, 12, 66.
Ovia, 38.

Palm oil, 20.
———— wine, 18.
Pawning, 97.
Phonograph records, 158.
Photographs, 153.
Political organisation, 11.
Polygyny, 15, 150.
Posthumous child, 68, 76, 85, 88.
Pottery, 22.
Prescription, 91.
Private property; *see* Land, Trees, Water.
Purification, 35, 41.

Reciprocal, definition of, 142, *cf.* 151.
Religion, 24.
Responsibility, joint, of family, 105, 107.

Rest day, 18.
Ritual, 30, 37.
River god, 32.
Road closed, 32.

Sacrifice, 29, 31, 33, 35, 43, 52, 78, 106.
Sass-wood, 111.
Seclusion of women, 29, 60.
Second marriage, 50.
Secret Societies, 38.
Sexes, proportion of the, 14.
Sickness, origin of, 24.
Silent trade, 19.
Sky-god, 26.
Slavery, 98 *sq.*, 100, 103 *sq.*
Social organisation, 11.
Solidarity, 105, 107.
Soul, 39.
Stolen goods, discovery of, 31.
Suckling children, 63.
Suicide, 42.
Suitor, duties of, 48 *sq.*
Supernatural, 27 *sq.*

Theft, 106.
Tolls, 19.
Totem, *see* Awaigbe.
Transcription, 123 *sq.*
Trees, 73, 94, 98.
Tribute, 11.

Uchure, 37.
Utu, 36.

Village, size of, 11.
Vocabularies, collection of, 128.

Water, 97.
Week, 18.
Well, 97.
Widow, 45, 47, 50, 68, 71 *sq.*
Will, 67.
Witchcraft, 34.
Witnesses to marriage, 57.
Woman's property, 68, 71 *sq.*, 76, 83.
Women traders, 19.
Women's cults, 32, 37.

Yams, output of, 17.

LONDON :
HARRISON AND SONS, PRINTERS IN ORDINARY TO HIS MAJESTY.
ST. MARTIN'S LANE.

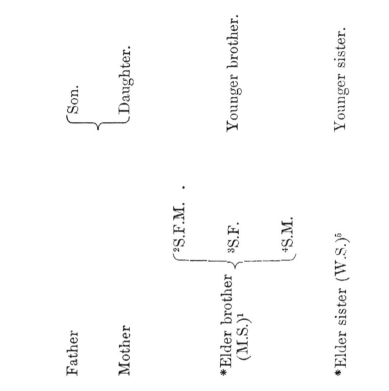

Father

Mother

Son.

Daughter.

[2]S.F.M. .

Elder brother (M.S.)[1]

[3]S.F.

[4]S.M.

Younger brother.

*Elder sister (W.S.)[5]

Younger sister.

INSERT
'OLD-OUT
OR MAP
HERE!

INSERT FOLD-OUT OR MAP HERE!

*Sister's son's child (M.S.) ...	Father's mother's brother.
*Sister's daughter's husband (M.S.).	Wife's mother's brother.
*Sister's daughter's child (M.S.).	Mother's mother's brother.
Father's father	Son's son (M.S.).
Father's mother	„ „ (W.S.).
Mother's father	Daughter's child (M.S.).
Mother's mother	„ „ (W.S.).
Husband	Wife.
Wife's father	Daughter's husband (M.S.).
Wife's mother	„ „ (W.S.).
Husband's father	Son's wife (M.S.).
Husband's mother	„ „ (W.S.).
Wife's brother	Sister's husband (M.S.).
Wife's sister	„ „ (W.S.).
Husband's brother	Brother's wife (M.S.).
Husband's sister	„ „ (W.S.).
Wife's sister's husband ...	

•Elder sister (W.S.)⁴ ...		Younger sister.
•Sister (M.S.)⁴ ⎧ S.F.M. ... ⎫ ; S.E. ; ⎩ S.M. ⎭		Brother (W.S.).
•Father's brother ... :		Brother's child (M.S.).
•Father's brother's wife ...		Husband's brother's child.
•Father's brother's child ...		
•Father's sister ... :		Brother's child (W.S.).
•Father's sister's husband ..		Wife's brother's child.
•Father's sister's child ...		
•Mother's brother ... :		Sister's child (M.S.).
•Mother's brother's wife ...		Husband's sister's child.
•Mother's brother's child ...		
•Mother's sister ... :		Sister's child (W.S.).
•Mother's sister's husband ...		Wife's sister's child.
•Mother's sister's child ...		
•Sister's son's wife (M.S.) ...		Husband's mother's brother.

¹ M.S., man speaking. ² S.F.M., same father and mother. ³ S.F., same father.
⁴ S.M., same mother. ⁴ W.S., woman speaking.

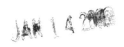